Getting back into
Amateur Radio

What's new and what you forgot

By Peter Parker VK3YE

Proofreading by Timothy Wallace www.ecologicmedia.com
Any remaining errors are the author's own

ISBN-13: 9781 5207 6710 9

WELCOME

There are many books for the beginner to amateur radio. There are also many for the experienced ham. But there is little specifically for the person considering a return to the hobby after a spell away. This aims to be the book that ends the drought.

Reasons for dropping out vary. You may have had family responsibilities, a busy career, a less favourable home location or competition from other interests.

Some of you not just watched but shaped technological development. Your working life may have swung from radio to television, electronics to computing, analogue to digital or hardware to software. Components got smaller, colder and less handled. Electronics became integrated, programmable and driven by lines of code. If this was your job you either kept up, dropped out or got promoted to management.

There may be fond memories of an early crystal set, shortwave receiver or electronic kit. It could have set your course of study or got you a job. There might have been good times had on CB radio or the satisfaction of using something you built yourself. You may vow a return to radio or practical solder-melting electronics, 'after I get a bit more time'.

For more and more people that time has come. Reasons vary but could include retirement, retrenchment, injury, children becoming independent, divorce or a move to the country. With changed circumstances, you can now do more of what you want. A return to radio may be one thing on your 'bucket list'.

But what will you hear when you turn on after thirty or more years? Will it be like analogue free-to-air TV which is all snow due to the shift to digital? Or will your 'second coming' in radio be even better than your first?

It depends on what you do and how you make it.

You won't be alone if you do return from a spell away. Many of today's active amateurs did just that. Made richer by experience from other fields, they contribute heavily to on-air, technical and organisational activities. They too were almost novices again, relearning what they forgot and catching up on changes since.

This book brings you up to speed with what has happened while you were away. It gives some tips on what remains, what has declined and the new things captivating our interest. Plus there are pointers on getting your call sign back, reassembling a station and becoming active again.

I hope this book will assist your quest so you can better enjoy all of what amateur radio can offer today.

Peter Parker VK3YE

February 2017

CONTENTS

I INTRODUCTION

It was still the 'cold war'. The Space Shuttle was new. No one had heard of O.J. Simpson. Oh, and that was about the last time you were last on air. Other responsibilities and interests took over. You sold your gear and let your call sign lapse. 'Steam radio' seemed so old-hat compared to the new and exciting computers coming in.

But, like a recessive gene, the 'radio bug' remained, just waiting for an event or changed circumstance to bring it out again. Things like a chance encounter. An exciting new mode or application. Fewer work or family duties. Injuries. A relationship break-up. Or a move to the country.

Whatever the reason, you wish to get on air again. Possibly with equipment you hankered after but never could afford, or homebrew you never had time to build.

You are not alone; the airwaves are full of previously lapsed hams giving radio a second go. And they're loving it!

There will be a learning curve. Not only recovering what you forgot but also in catching up on all the things that happened during your time out. The latter is something those continuously active never had to do since they had the luxury of taking in changes as they occurred.

Getting back into Amateur Radio aims to make your journey a little easier.

We'll start with a quick overview of amateur radio as it is in 2017. That's followed with some tips on tuning in. It may be news to some that, though the experience isn't quite the same, it's now possible to sample the bands without even owning a receiver.

Licensing requirements did and still do vary between countries. I'll run you through what has changed and what is needed in the US, Canada, UK, Australia and New Zealand. If you're elsewhere I'll give some pointers that will likely apply in your country as well.

Relicensing is not needed if you've kept your call sign current, but there are still regulation and frequency allocation changes to know about. You may find your licence level grants you more privileges now than when you were last active.

Over the years we've gained some frequencies and lost others. The more significant changes are outlined. Morse and voice modes like AM, FM and SSB are still used while new digital data and voice modes offer additional possibilities.

The rest of the book is a quick-start guide to getting on air. Advice on equipment, setting up a station and making contacts is given. This is worth at least a skim-through even if you remember a lot from your last time on air.

One can't hope to cover everything in one short book. Fortunately, finding out about things is easier than the days where you had to find an old-timer with 50 years of QSTs. More tips to help you get you started finish off the book.

Getting back on air is a worthwhile quest. I hope you pursue and enjoy it. Your comments and questions are invited and can be left on the VK3YE Radio Books Facebook page

2 AMATEUR RADIO IN 2017

Amateur radio has changed a lot in recent decades. In fact it would be remarkable if it were not so. Being a technological and social activity, changes in these spheres naturally carry across to our hobby.

Some facets have become more popular while others less so. But the general concept – that is, you assemble a station and talk to people – remains. As does the experimental and practical element of building your own.

There is now greater variety in modes and bands. There may be a ham up the road but you will never hear them because they're on bands and modes you are not. Or they might be more technically inclined and rarely radiate a signal. Even their house isn't necessarily a giveaway if they only operate with concealed antennas, portable or mobile. Not everyone can (or does) do everything, and conversation on one band does not reflect the diversity of other facets.

A common question asked by those away from amateur radio is the effect of technology, mobile phones, the internet and social media on activity.

Certainly there has been some impact. Before cellular phones, having 2-metres FM in the car gave hams a mobile communication capability few others had. That novelty has waned and, although there remain many VHF/UHF repeaters, high usage has tended to retreat to a few frequencies in most areas.

However, new technology has also brought us smaller, cheaper and lighter equipment. A countervailing social force has seen more people wanting to 'get away from it all'. Marry these two and we have increased interest in portable activity from remote locations such as parks and hilltops.

Another big change has been the extent to which the internet has enabled aspects of amateur radio. Examples include its use to spread technical information, obtain parts or arrange activity amongst like-minded amateurs. In the 1980s we thought reduced component availability would make home construction of equipment harder. Little did we know the rise of eBay and people-to-people international trade would create abundance rather than famine.

To summarise, the general ethos is similar even though activities and modes have changed. More detail on these trends in later chapters.

3 GETTING A TASTE

For nearly 40 years from about the mid-1960s most amateur activity was like a 'secret society' that needed ownership of a special receiver to hear. The switch to single sideband and the disappearance of shortwave bands from regular radios reduced the chance people heard us.

We have now come full circle. It is once again possible for the general public to tune in with equipment found in the average home (or even pocket). This is via free online receivers set up by listeners around the world. Typically covering segments of HF, VHF and/or UHF, the spectrum is laid out on a screen (below). Each signal causes a peak that you click on to hear. After setting mode and bandwidth, you fine-tune with your mouse to resolve it. This way you can hear what the bands sound like without buying a receiver.

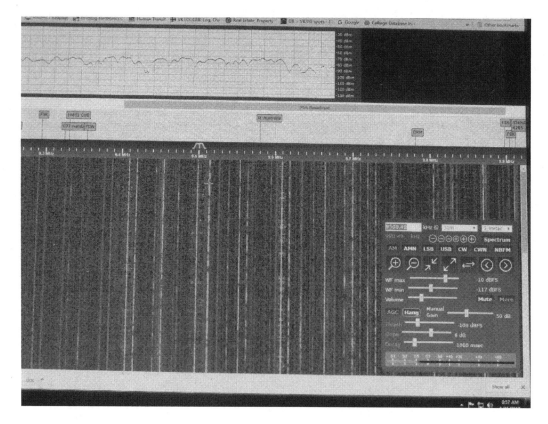

Hundreds of receivers spread all around the world can be found via websites such as sdr.hu, globaltuners.com, or websdr.org.

Search your city or country for one near you. Alternatively, try a distant receiver for an idea of conditions and activity on the other side of the world. Even better is that when you get on air you'll be able to use one to check the strength and quality of your transmission compared with others.

Is reception as good as your own receiver? Possibly not, especially if you're in the country. Many online receivers have limited frequency coverage or use small antennas from locations with high RF noise. What is heard is not necessarily what you would hear on your own receiver. But this in itself is educational, as it teaches how propagation and reception varies from place to place. Online receivers are one of the biggest recent advances in amateur radio and experience with them is highly recommended.

Your own receiver

The next step is to get set up with your own receiving apparatus.

Portable shortwave receivers can still be bought new at low prices. Many of the cheaper ones still have an analogue dial. They are not always good for amateur listening as they often only cover narrow broadcast segments and lack the beat frequency oscillator required for amateur signals.

Another possibility is to look for an old radio at jumble sales, garage sales or in second-hand shops. Check its frequency range by looking at its dial or the chart on the back of the cabinet. A range of 6 to 18 MHz is good for general shortwave listening while coverage of frequencies just above 1.8, 3.5, 7, 10 and 14 MHz spans the amateur bands. The best and most active bands for casual listening to amateurs on a simple receiver are 7 and 3.5 MHz with some areas also having activity on 1.8 MHz.

Be aware that you will need a beat frequency oscillator (pictured below) and tuning in amateurs will be a challenge, especially at higher frequencies. Don't pay more than a few dollars for an old radio and ignore vendors who claim a radio is 'vintage' or 'rare' and wish to charge dearly.

More usable are receivers with more bands, digital tuning and an inbuilt beat frequency oscillator. With typical coverage from a few hundred kilohertz to 30 MHz, they allow amateurs to be more easily received.

Cheaper receivers of this type may suffer internally generated noise and 'chug chug' tuning that makes fast band tuning difficult. Selectivity and the ability to reject strong out-of-band signals may also be sacrificed. Nevertheless amateurs should still be audible, particularly if an antenna better than the supplied telescopic whip is connected and you're away from local interference sources.

Suitable receivers are available new or second-hand. Hamfests ('radio rallies' in the UK) often have them at low prices. They also pop up on eBay but beware of paying too much. 'Rare' or 'collector's item' (especially for something of which thousands were manufactured) are red-flag words that indicate the seller may have inflated price expectations. You should be able to buy better than that!

A popular receiver good for casual HF shortwave and amateur listening is the Sangean ATS-909. This is less sensitive than some other receivers when only its telescopic whip is used. However, it performs well with a short wire antenna and is less prone to overload on strong signals.

Much older and made in large quantities is the Radio Shack/Tandy DX160. These are more than 40 years old. Many amateurs scoff at them but they provide tolerable reception provided you can tolerate a bit of drift. Just don't pay too much, since new SSB-equipped receivers (discussed next) have come down in price and are cheaper than what some still ask for drifty 30 to 50-year-old equipment.

Newer models include sets with brands such as Sangean and Tecsun. Key features to look for include continuous coverage up to at least 30 MHz, digital tuning in fine steps, and a beat frequency oscillator for SSB. As an example of what is available, below is a listing from a local distributor of Tecsun.

Tecsun PL660 Radio with VHF Air Band

$179.00

Buy Now

Tecsun PL600 World Band Radio

$129.00

Buy Now

Tecsun Shortwave and AM Outdoor Antenna

$129.00

Buy Now

Intek AR-109 Airband Scanner Radio

$125.00

Buy Now

Tecsun PL365 Multiband Radio

$88.00

Buy Now

Tecsun PL310ET Multi-Band Radio

$80.00

Buy Now

(source: tecsunradios.com.au - information subject to change)

Receiver reviews can be found on websites like eham.net.

You may have a yearning to build your own receiver. This can be a fun approach, especially if you're already into electronics or restore vintage radios so already have the parts needed. A simple regenerative, direct conversion or software defined receiver is a good place to start and makes an excellent weekend project. Numerous circuits, web articles and YouTube videos on these are available, with the regenerative set below a typical example.

Modern homes have so much interference from switch-mode power supplies and computers that, if heard at all, amateur signals picked up with just an indoor antenna are unlikely to be very clear.

An outdoor antenna is highly recommended. Something that's makeshift will get you listening. Or you could try reception from an outdoor location such as a park or beach. Even if you can only get a few hundred metres from the nearest house or power line, signals will be much better than at home. In fact, with a basic receiver and simple antenna in a good location you will likely hear more signals than with an expensive receiver connected to an indoor antenna inside an RF-noisy house.

16'5" to 50'

Five to 15 metres of wire in a tree clipped to a portable receiver's telescopic whip should work fine as an antenna. Wind it around a solder, rope or fishing line reel for easy storage.

HF activity

Good frequencies to hear HF amateur activity are the 3.5 to 4 MHz region at night and 14 to 14.35 MHz during the day. 7 to 7.3 MHz is often active day and night as a good all-round band. Exact frequencies vary slightly between countries due to differing regulations. Amateurs outside North America, for instance, usually have narrower allocations at 3.5 and 7 MHz.

With the receiver in SSB mode (LSB below 10 MHz, USB above 10 MHz for amateurs) slowly tune upwards from the lower band edge. Morse (CW) is still used and you may hear some signals in the bottom 50 to 100 kHz from the band edge.

Digital transmissions, such as newer computer-based modes, are often a bit above Morse. Finally, there is voice operation in approximately the top two-thirds of each band. Most of this is single sideband but you may occasionally hear older and newer modes; from AM to digital voice techniques. You may have forgotten how fiddly SSB is to tune. If your receiver has it, make use of the 'fine tune' or RIT control to adjust for the most natural voice.

Even though we are heading towards a sunspot low, amateurs should generally be audible most times you switch on. A listening session that is within a few hours of dawn and dusk will often provide the greatest choice of signals on a wide range of frequencies. Weekends tend to be more active than weekdays as more hams are out and about and nearly all contests are scheduled then.

Certain frequencies are better for particular distances than others. For example, 3.5 MHz is good for up to about 500 km at night but much less (and probably empty) during the day. In contrast, 7 MHz works well up to about 1000 km during the day and 3000 km at night. 14 MHz is very poor close in but gives good results beyond about 1000 km during the day. Really long distances – i.e. 15,000 km DX – may sometimes be audible for a few hours after sunrise and before sunset. Similar patterns apply for the bands up to 28 MHz with propagation available for progressively shorter times with rising frequency.

Many HF amateurs enjoy digital modes as well as CW (Morse) and SSB voice. As a listener you can eavesdrop on the otherwise unintelligible with free or very cheap software.

Audio from your HF receiver is fed into your computer's sound card. With the right program enabled, you will see text or images on the screen. Beacon modes like Weak Signal Propagation Reporter (WSPR) enable you to appear as a receiving station, with results of reception automatically appearing on a map-based website.

Some digital modes are very power-efficient. While their data transmission rate is too slow for conversation purposes, they can demonstrate that worldwide paths may exist on unexpected frequencies even with milliwatts of power. More on these modes in later chapters.

Something is probably wrong if you don't hear amateurs at all. Before giving up, tune to other frequencies to see what is audible. The WWV and WWVH time signals on 2.5, 5, 10 and 15 MHz and can be heard around the world with your receiver set to AM. They comprise pips each second and voice announcements each minute. Non-amateur HF SSB activity of interest includes inland communications, citizens band activity around 27 MHz, and shipping weather forecasts.

Here in Australia we have an annual yacht race between Sydney and Hobart where vessels call back on HF after a weather report. And, particularly in Europe and North America, HF pirate broadcasters may sometimes be heard using AM or SSB around 6 or 7 MHz. Pirate listening has become a hobby in its own right, with heightened activity on certain public holidays.

Although there is less of it than there used to be, shortwave broadcasting remains around 2.3, 3.2, 4, 5, 6, 7.3, 9.8, 11.7, 13.8, 15.2, 17.6 and 21.6 MHz. Signals should be heard on at least two or three of these bands at most times, with most stations around dawn and dusk. Failure to hear anything intelligible indicates a badly adjusted receiver, poor antenna, noisy location or the occasional HF blackout.

VHF/UHF activity

Maybe your prior radio activities were in the VHF and UHF range and you'd like to revisit activity there.

The first thing to note is that VHF/UHF scanning isn't what it used to be. The 1980s and 1990s were the golden years where VHF/UHF was full of police, fire, ambulance, aircraft, taxis, citizens band, couriers, business and other users, all audible on an analogue FM and AM scanner receiver. Most of this communication has since migrated to mobile phones or digital networks that cannot be as easily heard by the layman with a scanner.

Your old scanner is not completely useless but is limited to the remaining analogue users such as aircraft, marine, citizens and amateur users. Finding them is easier now, with spectrum regulators often putting their frequency databases online.

Terrestrial signals aren't the only reception possible; an old scanner and simple antenna may just be enough to hear amateur satellites transmitting FM near 145 or 435 MHz. Websites like amsat.org can assist with frequencies and pass times for currently active satellites.

Microwave frequencies, digital communications and computing multiply reception opportunities for the modern spectrum nomad. Exploration here requires something other than that battered scanner. But it can be an absorbing interest, as you pinpoint wireless data networks, detect local low-power UHF devices and trawl the microwaves from a local hilltop. Driven by wireless networking, security and recreational applications (think drones that transmit pictures to the ground), wideband digital microwave equipment has gone from expensive and rare to cheap and commonplace.

VHF/UHF SDR dongles

As for the receivers themselves, at one time only the well-equipped could hear much above 500 MHz. Now VHF and UHF receiving can be as close to your computer's USB port. In conjunction with freely available software, special USB software-defined radio dongles using the RTL2832 chip enable multimode reception across a wide slice of VHF/UHF. The spectrum display lets users see activity across a whole band segment, bringing a new experience only dreamed of by listeners of 30 years ago. Other SDR features include continuously variable bandwidth and digital noise reduction. Expect to pay about $US25 for one.

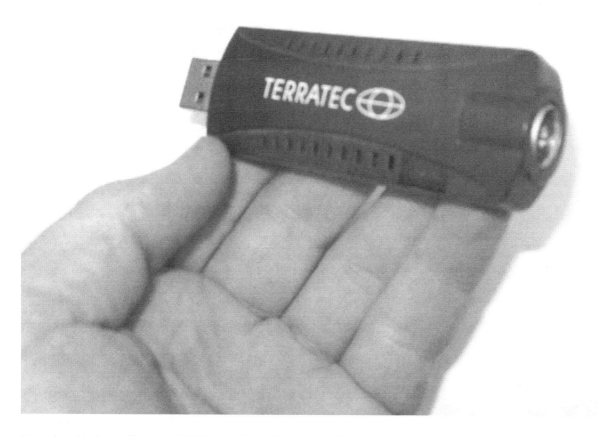

Despite its benefits, an SDR is still subject to all the problems of reception including overload from strong signals, internal noise and interference. Indeed its placement near computers can exacerbate these due to the broadband RF noise often radiated from switch mode power supplies, modems and monitors.

RF noise can be beaten through ferrite suppression chokes (slipped on to external leads that might otherwise radiate interference) and good outdoor antennas as far as possible from computers, home appliances and power lines. While receiver dongles sometimes come supplied with short whips, these are useless for anything but very local broadcast stations. Suitable antennas for SDRs are discussed later.

Upconverters for HF reception

We've discussed VHF/UHF reception with SDRs, but what about the below 30 MHz HF spectrum for international shortwave stations, amateurs and more? Cheaper dongles normally only tune VHF/UHF. However, basic HF reception capability is possible with a HF to VHF upconverter.

You can buy an upconverter preassembled or build one at home. Upconverters internally generate a VHF signal that is added to incoming HF signals in a mixer circuit to produce a sum signal in the VHF frequency range that the dongle can tune. An example is pictured below. Commercially-made units (search for 'SDR upconverter') are either separate converters or contain an integrated dongle that plugs into your computer's USB connection.

Overall performance can be quite good and you get features such as wide coverage, reception of multiple transmission modes, high frequency stability, variable selectivity and noise limiting that cheap stand-alone receivers lack. SDRs are particularly recommended for people with computing backgrounds returning to radio since it combines both interests.

Plug-in SDR downconverter

An alternative to a USB dongle receiver is a downconverter, which converts incoming signals down to the tens of kilohertz range. While not quite audio, such frequencies are low enough to be amplified and processed by your computer's sound card.

SDR converter

Antenna

RF amp

Mixers

**Computer with
SDR software**

Local
oscillator

Intermediate frequency
outputs applied to left
and right channel sound
card inputs (possibly via
external sound card).

The conversion is a mixing process somewhat similar to that described before for the HF to VHF upconverter. The difference is that you are converting higher frequencies to much lower frequencies. Also, you are using two mixers to feed slightly different signals to each channel of a stereo sound card. The effect of this is similar to 3D goggles, where slight differences allow a better discernment of depth. In this case it's small timing (or phase) differences which allow the SDR to be more selective and less responsive to unwanted signals on nearby frequencies.

Even though this description sounds complex, only a handful of parts is needed to make a basic SDR front-end capable of receiving a segment of one HF band (pictured below), and circuits abound on the web. If you prefer a kit, there are options such as the famous SoftRock kit, which has provided many with their first experiences with SDR. Best performance requires a high-quality sound card with stereo audio inputs, which in many cases is external to your computer.

Not all computers (especially laptops) have stereo sound cards. Will an SDR front-end still work? The answer is yes – but clarity will be inferior, signals will appear twice on the spectrum display and there is a large chance of interference from 'image signals'. Nevertheless it's an interesting exercise to try, especially with a very basic homebrew converter with only one output signal. In their crudity these are a modern version of the shortwave transistor radio plus broadcast receiver BFO combination that beginners used 30 or more years ago. However, the experience of interfacing accessories with computers and using SDR software to tune in stations is good preparation for using a better SDR.

Antennas

All SDR approaches require a good antenna for comfortable reception. An outdoor location in the clear provides stronger signals with less interference. I suggest having two antennas to start off; a simple vertical for VHF and some sort of horizontal wire for HF.

A coax-fed ground plane is a cheap but good choice for VHF/UHF. One with elements 48 cm long will work as a quarter-wavelength ground plane on 146 MHz in the amateur two-metre band. Although slightly away from optimum length on other bands (e.g. 156 MHz marine band where it should be 46 cm, or 130 MHz aircraft band where it should be 56 cm) reception on them should be fine. In addition, 48 cm is three-quarter wavelength at 438 MHz so can function for reception on the 70 cm amateur band and adjacent frequencies

50 ohm coaxial feedline is specified but if you have none lying around then TV-type 75 ohm cable should suffice. Thinner types such as RG58 are fine for short lengths. However, cable losses increase with frequency and thicker cable is better for longer runs, particularly if UHF (that is above 300 MHz) is your main listening interest.

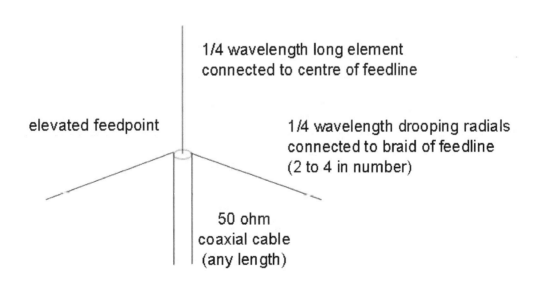

Generally there's a trade-off between antenna bandwidth, complexity and performance. An antenna known as a discone covers a large slice of the VHF/UHF band but is no better on any one segment than the simpler and lighter ground plane described above. Conversely, collinear (i.e. longer) verticals and yagi beams give excellent and sometimes directional performance on a single band with reduced performance away from it. More elements of different lengths can make a yagi into a broadband log periodic beam but, like a discone antenna, significantly more metal and weight is required for no increase in gain on any one frequency.

On HF, a coaxial cable-fed half-wavelength dipole gives excellent results on one band. It has a 50 or 75 ohm coaxial feedline with one quarter-wavelength piece of wire connected to the centre and another quarter-wavelength wire to the braid. The wires are spread out to appear like a straight line or inverted vee, with the coaxial cable feedpoint being the apex.

Thin insulated twin-lead, such as used for hooking up speakers, is cheap and suitable. A quarter wavelength on 7 MHz (known as the 40 metre band) is 10 metres and on 14 MHz (known as the 20 metre band) is 5 metres. Pulling the two wires apart provides the required half wavelength end to end.

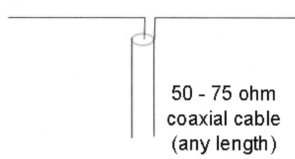

approx 1/2 wavelength end to end

50 - 75 ohm
coaxial cable
(any length)

A monoband dipole's only shortcoming is the loss of frequencies well away from what it was cut for. This can be overcome by having multiple wires coming off the one feedpoint. Precise cutting is required for transmitting but not for receive-only applications. For example, wires of 5, 10 and 20 metres long on each side of the feedpoint will work well on 3.5, 7, 14 MHz and several other bands where they happen to be odd multiples of a quarter wavelength.

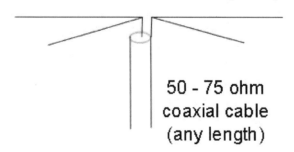

approx 1/2 wavelength end to end
on each desired centre frequency

50 - 75 ohm
coaxial cable
(any length)

Possibly the simplest HF/shortwave antenna is an end-fed wire. It's ideal for outdoors operation with a telescopic fishing pole support or convenient tree to throw it in to. At home, its main liability is interference pick-up since there is no shielded coaxial cable lead-in.

A wire between 10 and 30 metres long will work on most HF bands. An average height of 5 metres or more is suggested but it doesn't need to be perfectly straight or horizontal. By itself it will work well across the HF spectrum with a sensitive receiver. However, if your receiver is not so sensitive (e.g. a homemade set or simple software-defined radio) then a simple antenna coupler should be used between the wire and receiver to ensure most efficient signal transfer.

Below is a circuit diagram for a simple L-match antenna coupler suitable for use with an HF receiver or low-power transceiver. It comprises a coil (with connections every few turns to allow its inductance to be varied) and a variable capacitor that can be salvaged from an old radio. Values are not particularly critical, especially if you are mainly interested in the middle HF (i.e. 7 to 14 MHz) frequencies.

The coil can be 40 or 50 turns of thin insulated hookup wire wound on a plastic or cardboard cylinder approximately 4 cm in diameter. This can be from a clear wrap or aluminium foil roll. The insulation of one winding should touch that of the turns either side.

Every four or five turns the wire should be brought away from the cylinder, bent, and a small portion stripped. The exposed wire should be quickly coated with solder (to prevent the insulation melting) and the coil winding resumed.

The purpose of this is to provide tapping points for a small alligator clip (arrow in diagram below) so that more or fewer turns can be in the circuit. The purpose of this is to change the inductance to allow the most efficient signal transfer from the antenna to the receiver on different frequencies. If you have one, you could substitute an 8 or 10 position rotary switch for the alligator clip for easier adjusting.

The only other part needed is the variable capacitor. This can either be the large metal type from a vintage tube-type radio or a small plastic type from a transistor radio. The maximum value isn't that important provided it is between approximately 150 and 400 pF.

Often plastic variable capacitors (which you also sometimes see on eBay) have three connections because they contain two small capacitor sections controlled by the one shaft. The middle one may be slightly thicker and labelled 'G' for ground. It should be connected to earth on the diagram. The other two should be connected together to increase the total capacitance and thus antenna coupler tuning range. They then go to the antenna and alligator clip connection on the coil.

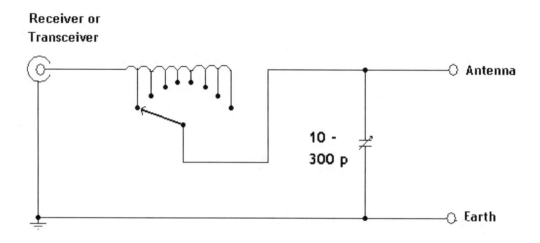

L-match antenna coupler

To summarise, hearing amateurs doesn't even require your own receiver these days, with web controlled remote receivers free to use. But I still recommend you set one up, whether as a stand-alone unit or software-defined radio. This ensures you get the full experience of building an antenna, tuning around, activity and local propagation.

Active listening

Like you may have done in your early listening days, I suggest spending an hour or so a few times a week slowly tuning across the bands. This may be at low, medium or high frequencies, depending on your interests. Note the time, frequency, signal strength and call sign of stations heard.

Then try to ascertain their location to get a sense of places that propagation favours most and least. Amateurs that have just established contact will usually exchange locations. Or you can look up licence details on your government's spectrum licensee database or the qrz.com website. QRZ is not 100% current but most active HF amateurs do keep their listing up-to-date and may include photos of their station. Other radio communications services, such as marine coastal stations, inland radio networks and broadcasting stations, will typically have frequency and transmitter location details on their websites. Shortwave pirate broadcasters (often around 6 or 7 MHz) are less regular but may use social media to announce their transmissions.

Your country's radio communications agency probably publishes a table or list of radio spectrum allocations. This shows the allocations reserved for broadcasting, mobile communication, low power devices, CB, amateurs and more. There will be some differences between countries, particularly on the lower HF, VHF and UHF bands which typically span shorter distances.

Within these allocations there will be more detailed lists, again produced by licensing agencies, enthusiastic listeners or radio organisations. These include AM and FM broadcast station lists and amateur radio band plans. The latter, promulgated by national radio societies, indicate where different modes are found within each amateur band.

Regular listening will familiarise you with propagation patterns and modern activity. If you have only a few minutes here and there, just tune a popular amateur band like 3.5, 7 or 14 MHz to sample conditions. Mix and match your listening times so you can see the regularity and variation of propagation conditions. VHF/UHF conditions do not change much between day and night but there can be some seasonal enhancements.

Time spent listening is worthwhile. By re familiarising yourself with propagation and getting up to speed with modern activity patterns, much less needs to be learned when you get a transmitter going.

4 GETTING RELICENSED

While some radio activities are possible without an amateur licence, getting on the air might be what you are really working towards.

If you've kept evidence of a past amateur qualification, you are often able to be reissued a call sign without having to sit any tests. It may even be possible to get your old call sign back if it's free. In some countries, holding electronic-related qualifications may exempt you from having to sit the technical parts of the exam.

In the 'worst' case you will need to resit exams. You may have forgotten many things but much will come flooding back after a small amount of study. Study manuals can be ordered from your country's national society and independent suppliers. Online guides, courses and videos can help as well. In addition, some countries have introduced easier entry-level licence grades so you can get in early and progress through activity. Links to websites that can help you find what is needed to study for your country's tests are given later.

Changes to licence levels and conditions may mean that you have more frequency, mode and power privileges than when you were last on air. The way exams are conducted may also have changed. Key worldwide trends over the last 20 to 40 years include:

* Conduct of exams. At one time these tended to be done by a single government authority, for instance the FCC in the US or the Department of Communications in Australia. Recent decades have seen exams done by many others, such as radio clubs and even individual amateurs (who may need to be accredited examiners).

* Morse Code testing. Once a requirement for amateur access below 30 MHz, this is no longer so. Things started changing about 15 years ago in many countries where HF became available to those who passed a 5 wpm test. A little later, following international agreement, countries dropped HF Morse requirements entirely.

* Easier or different entry points and privileges. The general trend has been towards easier tests and expanded privileges but there have been variations between countries. For example, the US and New Zealand removed their 'Novice' licences while the UK and Australia now have a 'Foundation' licence that permits low power operation on a range of bands. The requirements for the latter are basic; you can get qualified in a weekend course held by many radio clubs. As part of these changes, other licence

levels may have been renamed and granted increased operating privileges such as more frequencies, more modes and higher power privileges.

* Changing frequency allocations. Amateurs have gained from decreased government and commercial interest in the HF and lower VHF bands, with new and expanded allocations in many countries. For example, many countries have granted amateur use of segments below 500 kHz and there is a new amateur band around 5 MHz. Conversely, commercial pressures in the VHF, UHF and microwave region have narrowed amateur allocations in some countries.

* Fewer operating restrictions. Major trends in amateur radio have been the take-up of digital modes and the use of internet-controlled remote stations to take advantage of improved transmitting antennas and lower noise receiving conditions. Rules on these have relaxed in recent decades.

* Electromagnetic radiation (EMR) requirements. This is the one main area where regulation has tightened. Arising from public concern, regulatory authorities now require spectrum users to observe EMR limits. Standards vary between countries and are documented on regulator websites. In short, you must keep radio frequency exposure down in areas people can access. Modifications to your antenna, a taller mast or reduced output power may be required to ensure compliance.

* No licence fees. While there remain charges for exams and certificate issue, some countries have found collecting licence fees costs more than the revenue raised, so have removed the need for amateurs to pay. However, there may still be a need to periodically renew your licence to prove you're not dead. Amateur opinion on this is mixed; some claim to prefer to pay a licence fee in return for greater regulatory action on RF interference-causing electronic products or the small minority of amateurs who deliberately interfere with others.

Most countries have two or three amateur licence categories. Passing more advanced exams confers greater frequency, mode and output power privileges.

Summary licensing information for selected countries appears below. If your country isn't listed, find it via your national society's website (links provided later). Details can change so please verify with your local radio club, national society or licensing authority if important.

Australia (VK call sign prefix)

Regulator: Australian Communications & Media Authority acma.gov.au

National Society: Wireless Institute of Australia wia.org.au

Licence categories:

Australia has Foundation, Standard and Advanced licence categories, each offering successively greater band, power and operating privileges. Test elements include theory, regulations and practical.

Australian licence categories provide the following:

* Foundation: This is the entry-level grade introduced just over 10 years ago. It permits voice and Morse operation on 3.5, 7, 21, 28, 144 and 432 MHz bands with a 10 watt power limit. The power limit seems low but satisfying contacts are still possible, particularly if you operate portable and don't expect

international communication each time. Many radio clubs hold weekend courses for those wishing to get their Foundation ticket. Simplified theory requirements restrict Foundation licence holders to commercially made transmitting equipment. There is no past licence equivalent.

* Standard: Has exam requirements broadly similar to the old 'Novice' or 'Novice Limited' licence but offers many more privileges. Compared to Foundation licence holders, Standard amateurs enjoy more bands (3.5, 7, 14, 21, 28, 52, 144, 432 and 1296 MHz plus several microwave bands), higher power (100 watts on SSB), digital modes, a shorter call sign and the right to operate transmitters they build themselves. Benefits include more reliable communication and participation in nearly all facets of amateur radio. If you can provide evidence of having an old amateur qualification, the chances are you will get at least a Standard licence.

* Advanced: The current version of the old 'Full', 'Intermediate', 'Combined' or 'Limited' categories. It offers all Australian amateur privileges. Key attractions include access to some quieter but interesting LF, MF and HF bands (e.g. 136 and 472 kHz, 1.8, 10, 18 and 24 MHz), DX sections of 3.5 and 50 MHz, a 400 watt SSB power limit and a wider choice of call signs. Advanced frequency and power benefits will be particularly attractive for international communications in the next few years as sunspot numbers drop and HF activity moves to lower frequencies.

Call signs: The VK prefix and state numerals remain but there is greater variety in suffixes. Most notable are four letter VK//F*** call signs for Foundation licence holders. You may be able to get your old call sign back if it is currently unallocated. Further information is contained on the 'Guide to Callsigns' section of the WIA website.

Licence fee: $52 per year

Canada (VA, VE, VO, VY call sign prefixes)

Regulator: Industry Canada ic.gc.ca

National Society: Radio Amateurs Canada rac.org.ca

Licence categories:

Canada's licensing system is based on two exam papers but three categories.

A bare pass of the Basic paper allows operation above 30 MHz with a 250 watt limit. Such VHF/UHF frequencies are good for clear local communication, with SSB and digital modes allowing routine contacts out to several hundred kilometres. Even longer distances are possible when band conditions are enhanced or you are operating through an internet linked repeater station.

Access to lower frequency bands is given if you have a pass in 5 wpm Morse or gain a mark of at least 80% in your Basic Test (referred to as 'Basic with Honours'). The latter is good for communicating worldwide due to its generous frequency allocations and power limits. However, the technically minded will find a Basic licence restrictive due to its prohibition on homebrew transmitting equipment.

Full amateur privileges in this and other areas will require an Advanced licence, which also features a higher RF output power limit. Earning one requires passing the second, more advanced test.

Call signs: VA, VE, VO and VY prefixes. States and territories are numbered.

Licence fees: Canada charges no annual licence fees for radio amateurs.

New Zealand (ZL call sign prefix)

Regulator: Radio Spectrum Management rsm.govt.nz

National Society: New Zealand Association of Radio Transmitters nzart.org.nz

Licence categories:

NZ has a simple licensing system with one test and one certificate (the General Amateur Operator's Certificate of Proficiency). You need to hold this for three months and log 50 contacts on other bands before being granted access to frequencies between 5 and 25 MHz. Otherwise privileges are quite generous, including all modes and a 1 kW power limit.

The old 'General Class I' (12 wpm Morse) and 'Technician Class II' (no Morse) categories translate to today's General licence. There used to be a 'Novice' category (Class III) that had basic theory and regulations with a 5wpm Morse test but this is no longer offered.

Call signs: ZL prefix. Provision for both permanent and temporary call signs (e.g. for special events or contests).

Licence fees: No annual licence fee applies.

United Kingdom (G, M, 2E call sign prefixes)

Regulator: Ofcom ofcom.org.uk

National Society: Radio Society of Great Britain rsgb.org

Licence categories:

The UK, like Australia and the US, has three licence categories. All levels offer generous frequency allocations. Higher output power privileges provide the greatest reason to advance.

* Foundation: This beginner category provides access to many bands, with a 10 watt output power maximum. This is sufficient to be heard around your county on VHF and around Europe on HF. Longer distance contacts are possible but are much less routine. Foundation licence holders are not permitted to build their own transmitting equipment from scratch but, unlike in Australia, can assemble a kit.

* Intermediate: Allows access to all modes on almost all bands with a 50 watt power limit. This is much better than 10 watts when conditions are marginal or you are battling with compromise antennas. Another benefit is being able to design and build your own transmitting gear.

* Full: Gives access to all modes on all bands at full legal power. This includes being able to turn standard HF transceivers up to their maximum 100 watts without guilt. Full licence holders also have a G or M series call sign prefix which is better for DXing than the 2 prefix allocated to intermediate holders. The Full licence replaces the old 'Class A' (12 wpm Morse – all bands) and 'Class B' (No Morse – VHF and up) categories.

Call signs: There is a high chance of being able to get your old call sign back as the UK generally does not reallocate amateur call signs (unlike many other countries).

As background, older call signs started with G, with GI for Northern Ireland, GM for Scotland and GW for Wales. Later use was made of M and 2 prefixes. Currently issued Foundation call signs start with M6 (or MI6 for Northern Ireland, MM6 for Scotland and MW6 for Wales). Intermediate call signs start with 2E for England, 2I for Ireland, 2M for Scotland and 2W for Wales. Advanced call signs are M0 with regional prefix letter variations as per Foundation licences.

Licence fees: No annual licence fee applies.

United States (A, K, N, W call sign prefixes)

Regulator: Federal Communications Commission fcc.gov

National Society: American Radio Relay League arrl.org

Licence categories:

The US has three current licence categories: Technician, General and Extra. All have generous output power limits. Access to more frequencies and shorter call signs provide the main reasons to advance.

A General licence requires passes in both the Technician and General test elements. An Extra requires Technician, General and Extra. You can sit all three tests in the one session for no extra charge. Doing this is recommended even if you are not sure you will pass all elements.

More details on each licence type are as follows:

* Technician: Largely a 28 MHz and up licence with Morse-only privileges on narrow HF segments at 3.5, 7 and 21 MHz. If your interests lie in the VHF/UHF bands, this is all you need. However, almost all HF operators will want at least General.

* General: Includes all Technician privileges plus access to segments of all LF, MF and HF bands. All mode operation and a 1.5 kW output power limit is offered.

* Extra: Permits full US amateur privileges, including all bands, all modes and the full legal output power. Its main advantage over the General is access to HF frequencies that are popular with foreign voice and Morse operators. This makes Extra Class desirable if you're interested in worldwide communication on the busiest HF bands.

At one time there were other amateur licence types. You might recall, or have held, a 'Novice', 'Technician Plus' or 'Advanced' licence. Existing licensees kept those privileges but they were made unavailable to new applicants.

Existing and superseded licence categories largely sprung from the controversial 'incentive licensing' changes of the 1960s. These required some amateurs to sit more advanced tests just to retain their privileges and gave the US the world's most complex amateur licensing system.

Other changes came later. Novice licence holders regained VHF and voice privileges in the late 1980s under 'Novice Enhancement'. A little later a no-code above 30 MHz only 'Technician' licence was created. Existing 'Technician' licence holders, who had limited HF access due to their 5 wpm Morse qualification, became 'Technician Plus'. Later still, before Morse testing was abolished, the code requirement was lessened to 5 wpm for all HF licence classes including General (previously 13 wpm) and Extra (previously 20 wpm).

If you previously held an amateur licence, you may be able to obtain partial credit and not have to do so many tests. As an example, if you once held a General or Extra licence, you just need to pass the Technician element to regain your old licence class.

It is your responsibility to furnish evidence that you have previously been licensed. Historically minded amateurs have retained old printed callbooks and it may be possible to find yourself listed in one.

Call signs: US amateur call signs begin with A, K, N and W, possibly followed by another letter. Then a numeral followed by a suffix of two or three letters. Or they may have a single letter suffix if the prefix includes two letters. While in the past the number strictly indicated your geographic call area (typically a state or group of states) it is now possible to hold an 'out of area' call sign.

Call signs that you pick yourself are called 'vanity call signs' and can be applied for in exchange for an existing allocated call sign. Reasons for choosing a vanity call sign vary and include wanting one that reflects the holder's initials, brevity, ease of pronunciation or sentimental reasons (e.g. it being held by a deceased relative or 'elmer').

Licence fees: No annual licence fee applies.

Even if you don't need to resit an exam, you need to know current operating conditions to comply with your licence and prevent interference to others. The most important of these are bands, band edges, permitted output powers and band plans. Some will have changed since you were last on air. Regulations are discussed briefly next but it's essential to familiarise yourself with them through your licensing authority's website.

.

5 REGULATIONS

Operating restrictions

Overall, fewer and simpler regulations now govern amateur radio. Many countries have abandoned annual licence fees and the list of things you can't do is shorter. For instance, requirements to keep a log or get permits for portable operation have been removed or relaxed. There is more freedom with regards to unattended operating, digital modes and connection to the internet or telephone system. Fewer countries require you to change your call sign if you move to another call area. Entry level licensing has generally become easier with qualification sometimes possible in a weekend course.

Because amateurs obtain spectrum access for a fraction of what commercial users pay, we remain strictly non-commercial. That is, communication is personal and not for business purposes. Advertisements or entertainment cannot be transmitted. Causing interference to other stations is also prohibited.

There are some areas where regulation has increased. The first main area is electromagnetic radiation. We must now avoid exposing others to excessive RF energy. This is achieved by keeping antennas away from people and avoiding excessive output power. Amateurs can do a self-assessment on their station, making use of freely available calculation information and software. A recent failure by Australian amateurs to understand electromagnetic exposure standards caused a high power trial to be terminated and their historically low output power limits retained.

Antenna restrictions

The second area of increased regulation, particularly for city and suburban dwellers, affects antennas and masts. High antennas improve signals on transmit and lessen local noise heard on receive. Public exposure to electromagnetic radiation is also reduced.

Unfortunately landlords, local councils, bodies corporate and home owner associations do not always see things the same way. City councils may have planning rules with height limits. Property titles and lease agreements can be even more restrictive, with fine print prohibiting any outdoor antenna. This is particularly the case in areas where underground power and cable television make an amateur's antenna much more visible than in the past. Hints on establishing an amateur station despite these rules are given later.

Frequency bands

There have probably been changes to frequency allocations since you were last on the air.

Commercial pressures have reduced our access to some VHF/UHF/microwave bands in certain countries. For instance, US amateurs lost part of their 220 MHz band while Australians lost part of 430 MHz. Some microwave allocations are also narrower.
On the bright side, decreased commercial use has widened our access to lower frequencies. For instance, many countries now have amateur bands around 2200 metres (136 kHz), 630 metres (472 kHz) and/or 60 metres (5 MHz). Also, reduced or reallocated shortwave radio and TV broadcasting has led to wider amateur allocations at 7 and 50 MHz, particularly in Europe.

Details for each country are too long to go in to here. See your national spectrum regulator's website for a list of current amateur frequency allocations.

Gentlemen's agreements and conventions

In most countries amateur radio has a 'self-regulating' ethos. That is, while regulatory authorities set band limits and licence conditions, amateurs, through their national and international associations, are thought best able to govern what modes are found where within a band.

On most of our HF bands we find Morse (CW) starting at the lower band edge and then a narrow segment for digital modes. Each digital mode tends to cluster around particular frequencies in this segment. Most of the rest of the band tends to be occupied by single sideband voice, with slow scan TV, digital voice and AM enthusiasts favouring a few spot frequencies. 28 MHz is wider, with segments for beacons (near the bottom end), satellites and FM/repeaters (at the top end).

The VHF/UHF bands are like 28 MHz but with wider FM simplex, digital voice modes and repeater sections. Some also have portions for beacons and satellites. Their CW and SSB segments occupy a few hundred kilohertz from 50, 144, 432, 1296 MHz etc.

Although in most countries amateurs can legally use modes outside their recommended segment, they have no reason for doing so. As the aim is to make contacts, common sense would dictate that you go where others using your mode would, which is generally the band plan recommended portions. Besides, some of our bands are quite wide, so tuning the whole portion of it would be a real chore if (say) digital modes enthusiasts were spread out across it rather than occupying a small portion.

Success will be greatest if you study the band plans for the frequencies and modes you wish to use. They vary between countries, so use one prepared by your country's radio society or association. US readers should also note that the plans are stronger than a recommendation; they are, in fact, FCC rules that form part of your licence conditions.

Somewhere below gentlemen's agreements are frequency conventions that do not have the status of being listed in a national radio society's band plan. These are typically 'centres of activity' promoted by chasers of a particular award, low power operators, AM enthusiasts and others. They mainly exist so that adherents of that special interest have somewhere to tune around if seeking contacts. Unlike band frequency limits and band plans, they are a 'nice to know' that experienced operators should be aware of.

6 MODES, BANDS AND ACTIVITIES

Operating interests and activities have changed in the past 30 to 40 years. There is more happening on some bands and modes and less on others. This section brings you up to speed with new modes and what has become of the older ones.

Activity by mode

All the amateur modes of 20 to 30 years ago remain in use today, though relative popularity has changed. SSB remains popular on HF. AM has some following, particularly on 160 metres and the lower HF bands. FM is most used above 29 MHz. Digital voice techniques have gained some use on VHF/UHF with repeaters for several modes now available in the larger cities. Experimenters are also using digital voice on HF but it remains less robust than SSB over a variable signal path.

A question I often get asked is whether people still use Morse code (or CW). The answer is they do, even though it is no longer a licence requirement for HF. Morse is particularly effective for weak-signal, long-distance and low-power communication.

Easily set-up computer-based non-voice digital modes have seen the biggest growth. These range from modes you can hold a conversation with (e.g. PSK31) to those which, due to their slow transmission speed, are effectively a beaconing system (e.g. WSPR).

Further details on popular modes are below.

SSB

Many amateurs have settled on HF single sideband as their favourite interest within the hobby. Activities are diverse and include casual chatting, DXing (long distance communication) or radio contesting. The operating pace tends to be more leisurely on the lower HF bands and faster on the higher HF bands, especially if working rare DX stations.

An HF SSB station on a band combination like 40 and 20 metres can give a good range of local and long-distance contacts. Contacts are easy to come by and there won't be many times when you will be unable to work someone somewhere. In densely populated areas like Europe, SSB's popularity can lead to crowding and cause some to try other bands or modes.

SSB is also effective on VHF/UHF. While fewer VHF operators use SSB than FM, its adherents find it more rewarding. This is because, without repeaters, results on SSB are entirely due to your location, station, antenna and operating capabilities. Work on these is rewarding and brings stronger signals, longer reliable distances and better chances of success under enhanced conditions.

VHF/UHF SSB is great for those who like portable operating, antenna construction and the vagaries of radio propagation. However, unlike the busier HF bands, there are many times when no one is around. Arranging your activity around local VHF/UHF nets, field days and contests can maximise the number and variety of contacts possible. Also keep an eye out for conditions that support long distance contacts due to Sporadic E, tropospheric ducting, auroral and meteor scatter modes.

DSB

You may occasionally hear a double sideband suppressed carrier signal. It's easier to generate than single sideband and is popular amongst those who build their own transmitters. If you've always yearned to talk to people on a simple cheap and portable HF transmitter you built yourself, then DSB is the mode for you. Numerous transceiver designs abound on the web and even kits are available.

DSB transmitters and their often companion direct conversion receivers don't necessarily talk to each other well. However, they communicate effectively with SSB stations (i.e. about 99% of others on the band). In fact, if you're on frequency and your signal is clean, most SSB stations you call won't even be aware of your extra sideband.

Compared to SSB equipment, a direct conversion DSB transceiver has a transmitter and receiver bandwidth twice as wide and a lower transmitter efficiency (due to the wider bandwidth). These are only minor shortcomings for casual operating on an uncrowded band. However, it is probably not wise to use high-power DSB on a busy band because you will be twice as wide as SSB stations. You can lessen the chance of causing interference by using a direct conversion receiver since this has broader selectivity including reception of the unwanted 'audio image'. Provided this is clear, your wider DSB transmission will not interfere with other stations.

AM

AM, the original voice mode, retains a keen following in parts of North America and Australia on the lower HF bands. Many adherents repair, restore or convert vintage 'boat anchor' equipment. Others build from scratch, either making 'old rig' replicas from salvaged parts or exploring modern techniques with high-efficiency switching transistors.

AM accounts for maybe 1% of HF phone contacts. Its devotees value the practical aspect and the warmth of its sound laced with evocative fading and phase distortion. It is most used for local and medium distance contacts on 160, 80 and 40 metres. Some areas may also have AM activity on 10 and 6 metres.

AM is less power-efficient than SSB or DSB. Some commercial transceivers do not have particularly good transmit audio, making it even less effective. While a little fading and phase distortion adds 'character', a lot (most notable on multipath or sky wave contacts) reduces readability.

My experience is that 7 MHz is the best band for AM during the day. Even with 1 or 2 watts output (such as from an FT-817) distances of 100 to 600 km are common, provided the receiving station is in a low-noise country location. 1.8 MHz, despite the compromise antennas most have to use, is also worthwhile for daytime ground wave contacts up to about 100 km. Signals are particularly strong if you can locate across water from the stations you're trying to work.

3.5 MHz AM is a mixed bag. Phase distortion and multipathing can make AM QRP unreadable at night, while absorption and local noise harms daytime communication. Possibly the best time for distances up to a few hundred kilometres is a few hours after sunrise or before sunset when the band is more stable than at night and signals are stronger than during the middle of the day.

AM activity is often regionally based. You may find groups and nets on specific frequencies. Alternatively, you can try establishing contact on SSB and, if signals are good enough, request a change to AM, since most HF SSB rigs also do AM.

If using a frequency-agile AM rig, you can even call SSB stations on AM. If your signal is good enough and you've properly zero-beated on their frequency, they'll understand you. Just remember to switch over to SSB to understand their reply.

FM

FM, like AM, is easy to generate and has a crisp, clear sound that requires no fine-tuning. It's particularly favoured for local communication on the VHF/UHF bands, especially in conjunction with repeater stations on high buildings or hilltops.

FM gear is now very cheap. A Chinese-made handheld transceiver covering the 144 and 430 MHz band costs under $US50. Performance might not as good as a 'name-brand' transceiver but it will get you on the air, especially if there are repeaters within 20 to 30 km of you. Compared to when you last used FM, there are probably more internet linked repeaters and a greater use of tone squelch (e.g. CTCSS) to open repeaters. Websites and mobile phone apps have lists of repeater locations, frequencies and access tones in your area.

VHF/UHF FM is great for keeping in touch with local hams and club activities. However, unless you experiment with facets like portable locations and antennas it can get a bit boring after a while. The high attrition rate of amateurs who start with FM handhelds is why I don't recommend it as the only mode to have. As mentioned before, SSB on VHF/UHF is quieter but longer travelling and more challenging, while HF offers near-continuous activity over a range of distances.

FM on HF also gets some use, particularly on 10 metres above 29 MHz. While less numerous than on 2 metres or 70 cm, there continue to be repeaters on 29 MHz FM. These throw in a touch of the unpredictable, especially during mid-summer when Sporadic E allows communication up to 1000 km or more.

My own experiences of 29 MHz FM have been mixed. It can be stunningly clear when conditions are good; it's amazing to work across the country with local signal quality. However, there are many more times when fading causes an FM signal to get hissy and drop out. SSB is superior in such cases since it supports contacts under the variable and marginal signal conditions often found on 10 metres.

Digital voice modes

Digital voice modes are now established on VHF/UHF. Specialised repeaters, some with worldwide links, operate in many cities. There are several different and mutually incompatible types so plain old analogue FM remains the 'lingua franca' almost everyone has capability for.

Digital voice usage on HF is much less and remains a minority experimental pursuit. While digital techniques work well for slow speed/narrow bandwidth data modes, their application for HF voice communication remains a field wide open to the experimenter. As typical with digital voice modes (and to a lesser extent analogue AM and FM), reception is clear when a good path exists but rapidly degrades when there is fading, multipath or phase distortion. Until this is sorted out SSB is likely to remain the more popular option on HF.

Morse code (CW)

CW retains a following especially for DXing and contesting. Though there doesn't appear to be as much domestic CW activity as there used to be, you can still call CQ on bands like 7 MHz and get contacts.

CW's old advantages remain. For example, it is a very simple mode to build equipment for. While not endorsed here due to its lack of frequency agility, poor receiver and low transmitter output power, a basic 7 MHz CW transceiver kit can be bought for about $US10 and soldered in an evening. Making contacts will be hard work but 500 km can be spanned with perseverance. Consider it the start of a journey, with each improvement providing better, easier and more reliable results.

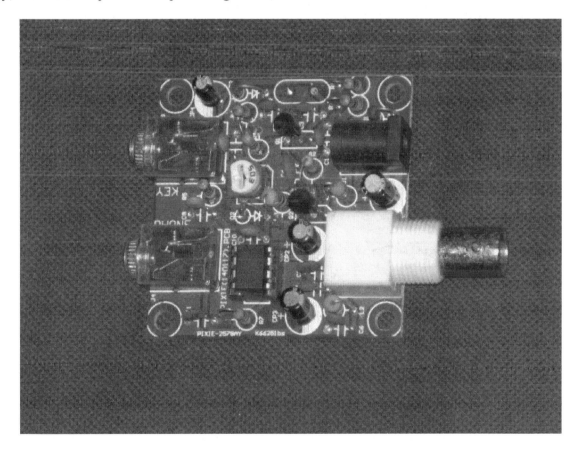

CW is more power-efficient for long-distance communication. This is of particular value when working people in locations with heavy interference, or if you wish to avoid an SSB contest taking up the rest of the band. Modern techniques being used by Morse operators include modern digital signal processing in receivers, software defined radios and the Reverse Beacon Network comprised of networked receivers around the world. Even if no one comes back to your CQ call, there's a reasonable chance a Reverse Beacon receiver will display your call sign and signal strength.

Slow-scan television

Regular television requires a wide bandwidth to transmit moving pictures. This bandwidth can be reduced to that required by voice communication if only still pictures are transmitted. Reduced bandwidth allows transmission on HF and thus international reception. This mode is called slow-scan television or SSTV.

SSTV pioneers used ex-war radar picture tubes. Enthusiasts built elaborate equipment and got excited when a grainy monochrome image appeared. From the mid-1970s manufactured SSTV cameras and equipment appeared. They were beyond the reach of most amateurs, however, and SSTV remained a minority pursuit.

All that changed in the 1990s. Computers got sound cards and cheap or free software became available. Like other emerging computer-based modes, SSTV transmission and reception became almost plug-and-play, with only a simple audio interface box (which can be made at home) required between computer and transceiver. You will very likely have all the equipment and parts required to get on SSTV without spending a cent.

14.230 MHz remains the centre of activity for HF slow-scan television. Online receivers let you watch activity received from around the world. If no one else is around, you can transmit your picture and see how well it gets through to remote stations.

Sites to visit to see live and recent SSTV images include g0hwc.com users.tpg.com.au/adslsymb/VK6AAL wb9kmw.com and hsiepel.nl/eur to name a few.

LIVE SSTV CAMS FROM AROUND THE WORLD

60 secs Refresh or Hit F5
Click on image to enlarge

The next step, if you wish to receive and transmit yourself, is to get some SSTV software. A popular option is MMSSTV, which can be downloaded from hamsoft.ca .

Your SSTV software will include various modes and speeds of SSTV transmission. On HF one of the Scottie modes seems to be most popular. When receiving, your software should be able to automatically detect which mode is being transmitted.

Crude SSTV reception can be done by holding the receiver's speaker up to the computer (or phone's) microphone. An audio interface box between computer and transceiver will give more reliable results. There's not much in them (transformers, level controls, transmit/receive switching) and they are either available commercially or built from circuits commonly found on the web.

The most recent development has been digital SSTV. This is transmitted on HF. Local groups in some cities may also be using it, possibly via a local VHF repeater, to swap pictures. Digital SSTV offers sharper pictures and higher resolution. Suitable software (e.g. Easypal and KG-STV) can be downloaded from g0hwc.com.

There are low-cost mobile phone apps that allow transmitting and receiving data modes when held up to an SSB transceiver. Provided you have a mobile camera phone with a screen good enough to be used outside, this can allow easy SSTV operation in the field. Examples are DroidSSTV and SSTV for iOS.

Radio teletype (RTTY)

RTTY has undergone an even more radical change than SSTV, with noisy teleprinters giving way to software and soundcards over the past 40 years.

At one time RTTY was the main keyboard chat mode, but this role has largely been usurped by PSK-31 (described later). It still has some enthusiasts and occasional RTTY contests continue to fill the band with teletype signals.

Packet radio (and APRS)

Amateurs active in the early 1990s will probably ask what happened to packet radio. Those years were its heyday. Its frequencies are much quieter now. Amateurs largely failed to embrace faster data speeds in the late 1990s, flocking to the then-new internet instead. A few still use packet but it's no longer the mass-interest mode it was 25 years ago.

A significant development is the marriage of cheap global positioning system receivers with packet radio to form the automatic packet reporting system (APRS). Position data from GPS receivers is transmitted via the packet radio system so that receiving stations can see where they are. In this way the progress of moving stations can be tracked on a map. Even if you don't have APRS it's possible to visit a web map interface so you can track the movement of APRS-fitted amateurs around the country. Further information on APRS can be found at aprs.org.

PSK31

PSK-31 (standing for Phase Shift Keying) has largely replaced RTTY as the popular keyboard-to-keyboard chat mode. It's efficient, easy to get going on and quite narrow in bandwidth. In fact, numerous contacts can take place within the bandwidth of a single SSB signal.

Like other modern computer-based modes all you need is a simple interface box (containing level controls and possibly audio transformers for isolation) and the appropriate free or cheap software, such as Digipan (via digipan.net) and MMTTY (via hamsoft.ca).

All you have to do is set your transceiver to the correct spot frequency (e.g. around 14.070 MHz on 20 metres) and watch the signals appear like waterfalls down the computer screen's spectrum display. Clicking on a waterfall puts you on that frequency for you to reply if desired.

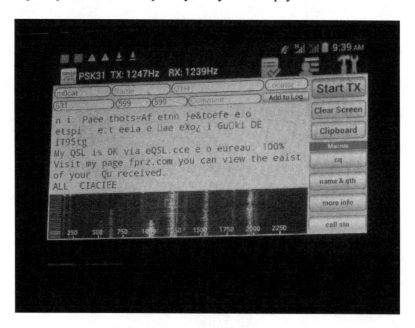

Before transmit, switch off your speech processor and ensure your microphone gain is wound back so you don't overdrive. Because PSK-31 (and many other computer-based modes) is full duty cycle, your transmitter output power should be reduced to about a third that used on single sideband to keep the final amplifier stages cool.

There is a certain magic to picking out readable text from a signal you can barely hear. And you may be able to monitor several conversations happening at once. It may be for these reasons that PSK31 and other digital modes are particularly popular amongst those running limited power and antennas.

You may also come across PSK63. This is a faster and wider bandwidth variant of PSK31. It's good for fast typists but is less power-efficient than PSK31.

Olivia

This is another digital mode that is robust under poor conditions. It is wider than PSK31, with its signal comprising a series of tones over a bandwidth of several hundred hertz. It is slow but still adequate for conversational usage. Details at oliviamode.com .

JT65

Slower but more robust than PSK31 and Olivia is JT65. It has excellent accuracy under weak signal conditions. It started on the VHF and UHF bands as an outgrowth of WSJT (discussed below) but is now also used on HF.

WSJT

One of the earlier ultra-weak signal modes, WSJT stands for Weak Signal by Joe Taylor (call sign K1JT), the mode's developer. It is widely used on VHF/UHF to cover marginal or long-distance paths not easily spanned with other modes. Thanks to modes such as WSJT, the use of the moon as a reflector of signals for worldwide communication went from being a minority interest requiring the highest of power and the best of equipment to something that much more modest amateur stations could achieve. Software and information is available at physics.princeton.edu/pulsar/k1jt .

WSPR

Some digital modes are so slow that you can transmit and receive but not have an actual two-way contact. An example is WSPR, or Weak Signal Propagation Reporter. It's basically a narrow bandwidth high-efficiency beaconing mode. Milliwatt signals span the world each day and you can visit the WSPRnet website to see who (including yourself) is being heard where.

WSPR has a fixed format where only your call sign, power output and crude location (based on the grid locator system) can be sent. It is a great mode for testing propagation at times when others aren't around, and for comparing the effectiveness of various antennas and power levels.

Because it takes two minutes just to send your call sign, a geographic grid locator and your power level, WSPR is not a conversational mode. Instead you leave your computer hooked up to your transceiver and check periodically whose signals you have decoded and who has detected yours. You will be amazed at the worldwide paths possible on bands thought to be dead.

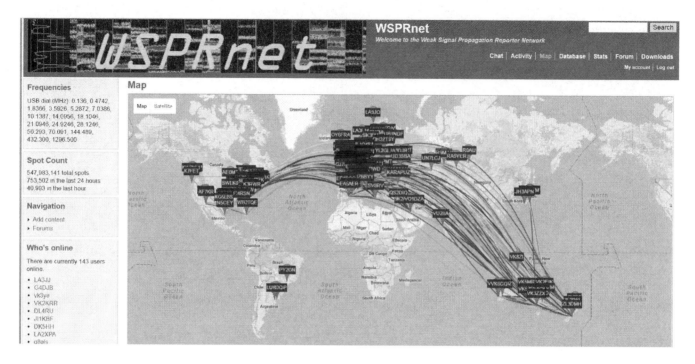

WSPR activity occurs on most amateur bands. Due to its ultra-narrow bandwidth and timed transmissions, numerous signals share a few hundred hertz. A simple (but stable) receiver wired to an internet-enabled computer with some simple software (available at dev.wsprnet.org/drupal) is all that is needed to set up a worldwide receiving and reporting station.

Getting started is similar to PSK31 or SSTV and the same interface box can be used. You could even get by watching the clock and manual transmit/receive switching for your first transmissions. But eventually you'll tire of this and want an automatic arrangement.

If you don't want to tie up your main transceiver for WSPR you can use simple dedicated transceivers instead. Further details on these approaches can be found on the websites of W3PM (knology.net/~gmarcus), G0UPL (hanssummers.com) and SOTABeams (sotabeams.co.uk).

QRSS

QRS is the Q-code for 'sending slower' on Morse code. QRSS is the name given to even slower Morse. So slow that instead of being decoded by ear it is decoded by computer or visually on a screen. Such prolonged dots and dashes allow reception under low signal levels, provided, like WSPR, you are content not to have a conversation. Common receiving software used include Argo, Spectran and Spectrum Lab.

Similar to SSTV, many amateurs have set up online 'QRSS grabbers'. Here you can send a signal and see if it shows on the receiver's screen. A QRSS grabber aggregator is a website simultaneously showing receivers from around the world. An example is at vk4yeh.com/qrss_grabber.htm.

Activity by band

A 90-year-old trend is for commercial and government spectrum users to make more use of higher frequencies and less use of lower frequencies. Amateurs, motivated by what they enjoy rather than what does a particular job cheapest and most reliably, have remained on both low and high frequencies. As others abandoned lower frequency bands, we gained expanded access.

No longer is 1.8 MHz our lowest band. Many countries have amateur allocations around 472 and even 135 kHz. At the other end of the spectrum, cheap surplus and ex-satellite gear has spurred interest on the gigahertz bands.

Interest in the HF bands swings with the solar cycle. We are currently on a downswing from a weak peak. There are still DX openings on the higher frequency HF bands but they will get less frequent and shorter over the next few years. Ways to get around this include exploiting mid-summer and mid-winter Sporadic E propagation (which happens regardless of sunspots), moving to lower (or very high) frequencies or using efficient digital modes. Although you don't have the same human experience of talking to people, automated modes such as WSPR can at least indicate that a path exists.

Less commented on but still important is what happens to lower HF bands during sunspot lows. Most dramatic is that bands like 7 MHz, which previously supported continuous blanket communication out to about 800 km during the day (and over 2000 km at night), develop a skip zone – a range of distances where signals skip right over. Signals on such paths become weak or drop out entirely. This is most notable at night (when there is also interference from longer distances) but is also apparent during the day.

To work stations within 7 MHz's skip zone you must drop to a lower frequency. 5 MHz may work where available. Alternatively, 3.5 MHz may be able to support communication up to 200 or even 300 km during the day. The reason that most urban amateurs hear nothing on 3.5 MHz during the day is high local noise and high absorption. However, quiet portable locations can overcome the former while absorption declines in low sunspot years as the critical frequency drops.

Even 3.5 MHz can fail to support short-distance communication at night when solar activity is at minimum levels. Your alternatives include 1.8 MHz (with its more difficult antenna requirements) or even VHF SSB.

Independent of sunspot cycle variations, there have been long-term changes to activity patterns. For example, when I started in the 1980s 3.5 MHz was very active, with contacts every few kilohertz each night. Today the band is much less active.

In contrast, more is heard on 40 metres (or 7 MHz). Shrinking gardens, licensing changes, wider frequency allocations and less interference from shortwave stations are some reasons for this. Also contributing has been the availability of kit transceivers, more portable operating and often associated awards and contests. 40 metres on weekends can now be almost as active as 80 metres used to be at night. It is a good all-purpose band, though as sunspot numbers diminish you will still want a 3.5 MHz capability for times when 7 MHz closes for some distances.

The dominant DX band continues to be 20 metres (14 MHz). Higher bands like 15 metres (21 MHz) and 10 metres (28 MHz) have devotees but recent sunspot peaks have been weaker than those of 1979, 1990 and 2001. Still, the twice-yearly Sporadic E seasons provide some rewarding contacts; and if your transceiver covers 10 and 6 metres it's worthwhile having an antenna for these bands, even if only simple verticals or dipoles.

10, 18 and 24 MHz (i.e. 30, 17 and 12 metres) offer a more leisurely pace ideal for those wishing to escape the frenzy during major weekend contests that clog the wider bands. 30 metres is a particular haven for Morse and digital mode operators, since most countries prohibit SSB due to the band's narrowness. Its propagation characteristics, which are a curious mix of lower and higher HF bands, make 30 metres open to somewhere at almost all times.

The above is a summary of activity on just some of the bands available to us. More detail on each band is presented below.

Band characteristics (adapted from *Minimum QRP*)

The summaries below describe the characteristics of the various amateur bands. The impressions should hold for most mid-latitude countries around the world, though activity levels will vary with population density. They have been compiled from nearly 30 years of listening in Australia and more recent use of web-based receivers around the world.

135 kHz (2200 metres) and 472 kHz (630 metres)

Allocations around the world vary. Many countries such as Australia have allocations around 136 and 472 kHz. In contrast the US has a non-amateur 'LOWFER' segment around 160 kHz that anyone can use provided they keep effective radiated power down.

Narrow bandwidth and long wavelengths are the two distinguishing features of bands in this area. The narrow bandwidth means that most if not all activity will be CW and digital modes rather than SSB. The long wavelength means excellent ground wave coverage but inefficient antennas unless they can be made very large. The two work against each other but there are some distances where 472 kHz propagates better than 1800 kHz, even with a similar-sized antenna that is less efficient on the lower frequency.

Commercially made equipment is not known to be available so these bands are the domain of the homebrewer. While HF amateur transceivers sometimes receive on low frequencies, their performance here can be an afterthought. It may be better to build a simple LF to HF upconverter with a selective front end. More than on the HF bands, there are marked differences between transmit and receive antennas. Transmit antennas are designed for maximum efficiency while receiving-only antennas maximise signal to noise ratio. For the latter, a compact loop with a sharp null aimed at local interference is often employed, though those on large lots of land can experiment with a long Beverage.

Cheap audio transistors can provide good power at these frequencies, so moderate to high power transmitter stages are relatively simple. While builders may construct 100 watt or more transmitters, the inefficiency of antennas generally used means effective power output is a few watts or less.

1.8 MHz (160 metres)

160 metres is another band that attracts a devoted minority. It's perfect if you've succeeded on the higher bands and want a new challenge. Every DX contact on the band is hard earned and signals are often buried in noise. This makes 160 metres a rewarding haven for those who experiment with receiving, such as using low-noise antennas and interference-cancelling systems.

Stable day and night groundwave propagation makes 160 metres suitable for reliable local communication out to 50 km or more even with low power. This makes it much more like VHF compared to HF bands. It propagates extremely well over salt water and is superior over rough terrain. However, increasing RF noise levels in urban areas, poor mobile antenna efficiencies and the desire for handheld communications has forced police, emergency services, marine and cordless phone users to move to VHF and UHF.

Notwithstanding its abandonment by other users, the 2 MHz region remains interesting for amateurs who operate portable or experiment with kite antennas. 160 metres is also popular amongst AM operators, who may be using anything from restored 'boat anchor' gear, converted marine transceivers to ultra-simple homebrew rigs, often on popular cheap crystal frequencies such as 1843 kHz. Again, listening will reveal details of regular and casual activity in your area.

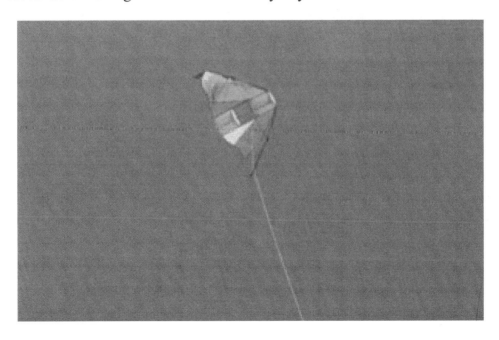

There is some cross-over with broadcasting, with many 160 metre operators having professional experience in broadcasting and taking great pride in the audio quality of their transmissions. This contrasts with the narrow 'communications quality' favoured on the more DX-oriented bands.

Builders of crystal sets and regenerative receivers find these work well on 160 metres. In some cases it was after hearing activity on that band that they became licensed amateurs. Consequently 160 metres, like 80, 40 and even 11 metres (27 MHz CB), has a special place in the personal history of many amateurs.

Good local groundwave coverage on 160 metres requires a vertically polarised antenna. A full quarter wave, which is prohibitive in most gardens, is not needed; capacitance hats and top loading can allow satisfactory performance from a short antenna.

Another mode, useful to cover areas just beyond the groundwave range, is close-in high-angle skywave propagation at night. This permits reliable communication up to several hundred kilometres with QRP. Because of the high radiation angle required, a low dipole may radiate better than a vertical antenna. Keen 160 metre operators can often switch between vertical and horizontal antennas for best results.

Finally there is the DX capability on 160 metres. 15,000 km DX contacts on 160 metres are rare but possible between well-set-up stations. An effective low-angle antenna is desirable on transmit but on receive low noise is most important. Hence the tendency for serious 160 metre operators to use separate transmit and receive antennas. Example receive antennas include a long wire Beverage or wave (for those with plenty of space) and a tuned rotatable loop (for those with limited space).

While higher HF bands like 20 metres may be open for long-distance QRP DX contacts over one to two hours or more, openings on 160 metres tend to be shorter. 160 metres DX propagation tends to be tied to the 'grey line', meaning most DX action is seen around sunrise and sunset and either or both ends of a path. Grey-line conditions change with season, so certain DX paths may best be workable at one or two times of the year only.

160 metre usage varies around the world. Tune around at various times to get a feel for activity before committing to building a dedicated 160 metre transmitter or antenna. If you already have a transceiver that covers 160 metres, consider a makeshift antenna to get a taste of the band. Examples include a higher frequency dipole with vertical feeders tied together and fed against earth, or a metal mast with beams shunt-fed with a gamma-type arrangement.

What you don't get in quantity of contacts is often made up in quality if you take the 160 metre QRP challenge. CW is most used for DX, SSB for up to several hundred kilometres, and AM for local nets in some areas. Digital modes such as WSPR also have a following. Equipment is easy to build for 1.8 MHz and audio transistors can effectively generate QRP power levels.

During the day, expect 10 to 50 km groundwave coverage and up to about 300 km close-in sky wave at night. QRP DX across any of the major oceans is quite possible on 160 metres, especially if operating portable from the coast and the receiving station is well skilled and equipped.

160 metres is an immensely challenging band. The distance and variety of stations easily workable is less than on some of the higher bands. Space for antennas, noise levels and local activity are the major considerations for those seeking to become active on this band. Unless there is considerable local activity, beginners are advised to first equip themselves for another band, such as 40 or 80 metres, before trying 160.

3.5 MHz (80 metres)

At half the wavelength, efficient antennas are easier for 80 than 160 metres. More amateurs in more countries are set up for the band and working DX is easier. Home to many regular club nets and skeds, 3.5 MHz is a popular choice for local and semi-local chatting in the early morning and evening. DX is difficult but still possible with modest antennas.

There are always swings and roundabouts when comparing the propagation characteristics of amateur bands. Groundwave propagation on 80 metres is much less effective than on 160 metres. Daytime skywave propagation on 3.5 MHz is thwarted by still-high D-layer absorption levels. This makes the band appear dead to everyone except those blessed with low RF noise levels.

With so few signals heard on 80 metres during the day, some think it is strictly a night-time band. This is an oversimplification. Around one to two hours after sunrise or before sunset are also productive times on 80 metres. SSB is a less efficient mode than CW but may produce more contacts due to generally higher phone activity.

Every ham should expose themselves to propagation vagaries by tuning all bands at various times of the day and night. As mentioned before, seldom is much heard on 80 metres between mid-morning and mid-afternoon.

Propagation slowly changes about two to three hours before sunset. Absorption drops. Signals just beyond groundwave range, from 100, 200, 300 then 400 kilometres away, become audible with strength gradually increasing. While indicated strengths may be less than at night, readability may be better due to less interference from distant stations or lightning storms. There are probably a few contacts taking place but the band is less busy than during the early evening peak period. Most contacts are regular skeds, made each day or week between largely the same people. Those you hear may seem entrenched in contact and few are heard calling CQ, particularly in the morning.

Initially this seems unpromising if wishing to make contacts. However, there are benefits operating at these times, especially in more populated countries. There is likely to be reduced static and crowding. Also your signal may stand out more if you do call CQ. If no replies ensue, some other ways to get contacts are discussed elsewhere.

Darkness brings more onto the band. That comes from locals turning on after dinner and more distant stations becoming audible. Signals readily span from several hundred to a few thousand kilometres, with these distances being easier than on 160 metres. Others may have to battle with interference from other stations or distant lightning storms but many enjoyable contacts should still be possible.

Most 80 metre operators are content to make contacts over the short and middle distances for which the band is most suited. Higher bands like 20 and 40 metres meet their appetite for DX. However, there are 'band loyalists' who stick to 80 metres through thick and thin, and in doing so work some amazing DX, even with low power. Such contacts are most likely on CW but even then are neither daily occurrences nor consistently readable. When they do occur, they tend to follow the darkness; i.e. towards the east after dusk and the west before dawn. North-south contacts tend to be possible over more of the night.

The critical frequency only occasionally drops below 3.5 MHz, even during sunspot minimum years. This gives the band a reliability that 7 MHz lacks for communication up to a few hundred kilometres. This trait makes 80 metres popular amongst mobile operators and campers who wish to maintain communication with friends in their nearest city. On those rare occasions where the critical frequency is depressed, the main alternatives are to try 1.8 MHz or reschedule the contact for an hour or two after sunrise or before sunset.

80 metres is a good choice for the operator wishing to make local and medium-distance contacts. Equipment is simple and easy to build. The large antenna required, noisiness and lack of daytime activity are the band's main disadvantages.

5 MHz (60 metres)

Only some countries permit 60 metres. It is generally shared with other users. Amateurs may only be able to operate under special conditions, for example spot frequencies, USB voice transmission or lower power limits.

5 MHz is an interesting mix of 3.5 and 7 MHz. Daytime absorption on 5 MHz is substantially less than 3.5 MHz. Even during low sunspot years 5 MHz is mostly above the daytime critical frequency. These characteristics put it in the 'sweet spot' for reliable communication up to about 300 or 400 km during the day. Such close-in contacts are often successful on 5 MHz at times when low solar activity only supports longer distances on 7 MHz.

As confirmed by consistent reception of the WWV/WWVH time signals on 5 MHz, nights should allow worldwide communication similar to 3.5 and 7 MHz. However, it may not always provide the blanket local coverage that 3.5 MHz mostly provides at night, due to the existence of a skip zone in low sunspot years.

7 MHz (40 metres)

7 MHz is perhaps the best all-round band for casual HF operating. Antenna requirements are modest and there are numerous kit and ready-made rigs available for the band. Effective communication is possible throughout the day, and a wide range of stations near and far can be worked. Its only downsides are that it can be crowded in populated countries and DX contacts longer than about 3000 km are difficult. Lightning static can also spoil reception in areas with high electrical activity.

A strength of 7 MHz is its convivial nature. Groups seem to be less tight than on 80 metres and stations calling CQ are more commonly heard. It is also less rushed and competitive than 20 metres. These traits make 40 metres an ideal band to attempt first contacts on equipment you've built or restored yourself.

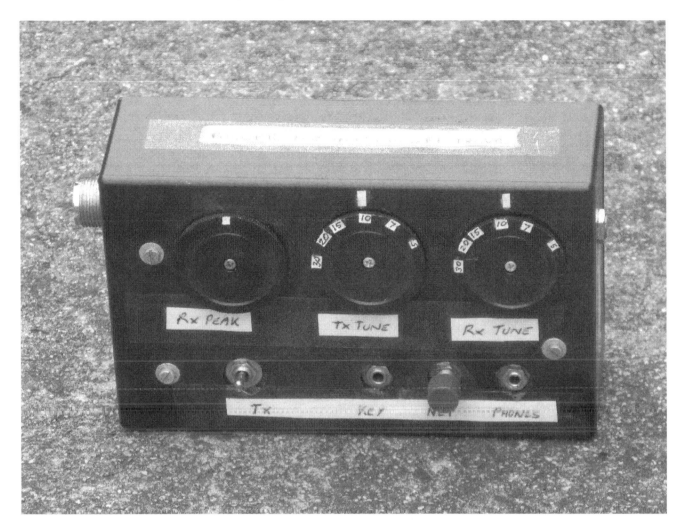

A modest dipole, inverted L or horizontal end-fed wire is enough to get started and will provide many reliable contacts on 40 metres. A wire antenna like this will fit into even modest yards and is easily thrown over a tree branch if operating outside. The medium and high radiation angles will allow numerous contacts out to about 800 km over much of the day. In medium to high sunspot years, the critical frequency usually exceeds 7 MHz. Close-in contacts, even within your own city, county or state, are both possible and easy.

At night, or during the day in low sunspot years, when a skip zone develops, closer-in stations get replaced by distant signals. Signals from 5000 or 10,000 km away are often tantalisingly strong at night. Don't be disappointed, though, if few hear your calls; 40 metres is the sort of band where you will hear many more distant stations than they will hear you, due to interference and static at their end. A more common maximum distance with low power on 40 metres is about 3000 km, especially if using a modest antenna with mostly high-angle radiation.

Having said that, long-haul DX on 7 MHz is sometimes possible. It just takes more skill and persistence than spanning the equivalent distance on 14 MHz. A low-angle antenna such as a vertical with a good ground system will increase your chances. It is even better if you are able to locate close to the coast for good contact with distant stations across the water. Like other low HF bands, 7 MHz is a 'darkness' DX band, with signals following the dark. This means that sunrise should see reception of distant signals from the west and sunset should allow reception over long distances to the east.

7 MHz is an excellent band capable of providing a wide variety of local and medium-distance contacts. Small antennas, reasonable activity, low noise levels, daytime propagation and comparative ease of building equipment all make it a very good choice for the newcomer or returnee to radio.

10 MHz (30 metres)

At just 50 kHz wide, 10 MHz is the narrowest available HF band and was only allocated to amateurs in 1982. Most countries disallow SSB, making the band a haven for CW and digital modes. By convention, 10 MHz, like 18 and 24 MHz is contest free, making it a welcome refuge for those fleeing contests elsewhere.

At the transition point between the lower HF bands and the high HF bands, 10 MHz has characteristics of both. It is open almost all the time to somewhere in the world, though exactly where can be difficult to work out. This trait makes 30 metres popular amongst WSPR operators who can leave their station going overnight and see where they have been spotted when they check in the morning.

Because the critical frequency is nearly always below 10 MHz, the band is much less reliable than lower frequencies for contacts of up to a few hundred kilometres in low and medium sunspot years. Hence its strength is with medium to long distance contacts. This contrasts with 7 MHz, which is better for short to medium range contacts.

The best time for worldwide communication on 30 metres is within a wide two or three hour period centred on dawn and dusk. At these times signals from most continents can be heard simultaneously and the band is at its busiest. Conditions vary at other times. For instance, 10 MHz may be too high to support much propagation at night when sunspot numbers are low. DX signals tend to drop off in the middle four to six hours of the day, but the band can still support effective communication in the 700 to 1500 km range.

I have found DX contacts harder on 10 MHz than 14 MHz. This may be due to my relatively remote location. You may find better results on 10 MHz. Things in your favour include less competition due to often lower legal power limits, generally simpler antennas and the absence of contests.

30 metres allows excellent medium to long distance QRP communication during much of the sunspot cycle over much of the day.

14 MHz (20 metres)

14 MHz is prime spectrum for HF DXing. During a major contest it gets used by thousands of stations simultaneously, so it can be hard to find a space or dodge interference. If you can handle the terse operating, where few contacts progress beyond signal report, name and location, 20 metres is the place to be to work the widest range of stations, from about 1000 km away to the other side of the world.

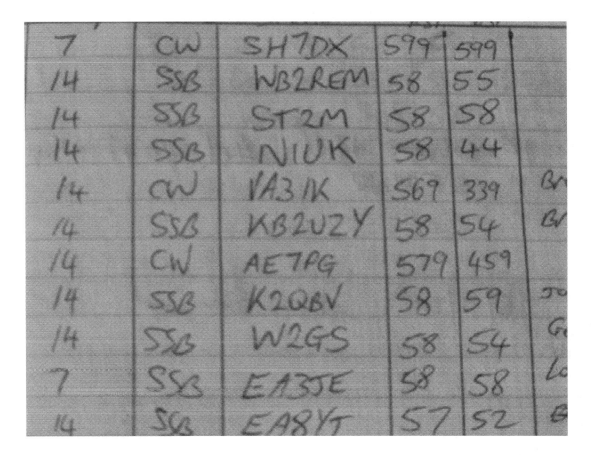

7	CW	SH7DX	599	599	
14	SSB	WB2REM	58	55	
14	SSB	ST2M	58	58	
14	SSB	N1UK	58	44	
14	CW	VA3IK	569	339	Br
14	SSB	KB2UZY	58	54	Br
14	CW	AE7PG	579	459	
14	SSB	K2QBV	58	59	Jo
14	SSB	W2GS	58	54	Gi
7	SSB	EA3JE	58	58	Lo
14	SSB	EA8YT	57	52	B

Like 10 MHz, the longest distances are more easily worked just after dawn or just before sunset. The band is normally open around midday but for shorter distances. 14 MHz generally closes at night, particularly during low sunspot years. Poor groundwave characteristics and a critical frequency almost always below 14 MHz means the band can only occasionally support short-distance communication.

14 MHz SSB is arguably the competitive 'bear pit' of amateur radio where a bit of transmitter power can be handy. Nevertheless, worldwide voice communication is still sometimes possible on 14 MHz with low power. You can more easily work the world with CW or digital modes, which are more efficient.

Slow-scan TV (found around 14.230 MHz) is also popular. Live SSTV webcams allow you to monitor your transmitted picture from around the world even if no stations are active to make a two-way contact. Software for both PSK-31 and SSTV is freely available. Transmission only requires a very simple interface box between transceiver and computer.

Notwithstanding crowding from other stations, 14 MHz is the ultimate band for the amateur wishing to work DX.

18 MHz (17 metres)

A step from 14 to 18 MHz can be rewarding if propagation is good. Operating tends to be at a more relaxed pace and the band is contest-free. Lower occupancy means a greater chance of picking a frequency not in use elsewhere and having adjacent higher power signals bleed over onto your frequency.

In addition, fewer stations have gain antennas for 17 metres than for 20 metres. This means that if you can erect a gain antenna, even if only a fixed-wire beam in a favoured direction, even a low power signal can often be clearly heard.

18 MHz is widely enjoyed as a relaxed alternative to 20 metres. However, it is less consistently open.

21 MHz (15 metres)

21 MHz is another band capable of excellent results, especially for north-south paths. It is wider than 14 MHz so is less crowded, even though contests are allowed. Its smaller wavelength makes gain antennas smaller and cheaper to build.

15 metres is most suited to those whose routines permit frequent daytime operating. The previous comments about volatility apply with even greater force for 21 MHz and upwards.

21 MHz is an excellent but volatile band highly dependent on solar activity.

24 MHz (12 metres)

24 MHz is a cross between 21 and 28 MHz. It is perhaps the least used HF band but this means your signal will stand out if there is a reasonable opening. There are times when 24 MHz is open but 28 MHz is not. It is most effective if you are in low latitudes and/or have large amateur populations on the other side of the equator from you.

24 MHz can yield good results when conditions are right. Just don't count on contacts if it is your only band.

28 MHz (10 metres)

28 MHz is a fun but fickle HF band wide enough to provide for a broad range of operating modes and interests. Antennas for it are small and easily built and the band can provide outstanding DX results in high sunspot years.

The band supports local communication up to a few dozen kilometres, similar to 27 MHz CB. Sporadic E provides contacts in the 1000 to 2000 km range in midsummer and midwinter at any phase of the sunspot cycle. Signals can be extremely strong and even mobile stations can have massive signals. Most local activity is SSB while CW gets most use for DX working.

FM simplex and repeater activity occurs above 29 MHz. Unfortunately, fading and phase distortion affects FM more severely than it does SSB. This makes 10 metres FM both exhilarating and frustrating – more often the latter. Enjoy the good propagation on FM but otherwise stick to CW/SSB unless you're only interested in local contacts, are near a 10 metre FM repeater or have excellent (beam) antennas.

28 MHz is capable of high-quality contacts when conditions are right. It can be very quiet when they are not. Hence it is not recommended as an only band.

50 MHz (6 metres)

50 MHz is like 28 MHz but with greater extremes. It provides effective local communication, comes alive in midsummer (and midwinter) due to Sporadic E, and opens up to intercontinental communication when sunspot numbers are very high.

Six metres is very much a gambler's band. Switch on at random times and chances are you will hear no one. However, it has been the medium of many 'once in a lifetime' contacts when open. Unless you're happy with midsummer Sporadic E contacts up to 2000 or 3000 km, success on this band requires constant monitoring of mostly noise.

Although the band supports good local communication, and some countries have 6 metre FM repeaters, the dominant operating culture on 50 MHz is SSB DX. CW is very much a minority mode on 6 metres but has provided many of the band's top DXers with rare and memorable contacts.

50 MHz is *the band for the operator who is seeking the ultimate DX achievement and willing to sit by the radio all day waiting for it to happen. There can be days if not months between contacts since there isn't the level of casual everyday activity found on most HF bands. For local contacts, though, 6 metres is an excellent alternative to 2 metres – if you can persuade others to use it.*

70 MHz (4 metres)

70 MHz is available in a few (mostly European) countries. Commercially made equipment is less widely available than for other bands. Propagation characteristics include excellent local coverage and summer Sporadic E excitement, but it is quieter than 2 metres.

144 MHz (2 metres)

144 MHz is the most popular of the VHF/UHF bands and permits a wide range of operating activities. CW/SSB is good for local and extended local contacts when 160/80/40 metres is noisy or you have severe antenna space constraints. Distances of 200 to 300 km are quite achievable with modest equipment from an elevated location.

Antennas on 144 MHz and up are normally horizontally polarised for CW/SSB and vertical for FM. The serious 2 metre operator should ideally have three antennas: an omnidirectional vertical and a vertical beam for FM, and a horizontal beam for SSB. Fortunately antennas are easy and cheap to build, with many parts available from hardware stores or even old TV antennas.

2 metre activity is regionally based. It tends to be less suitable for random contacts than HF; you may turn on and only hear a few repeaters or simplex frequencies active at any one time. On the other hand, local nets, contests, field days and activity sessions bring many out of the woodwork. Weeknights or weekend mornings seem to be the most common times. Time your occasions on the air to coincide with these and you'll have many rewarding contacts.

Long distance contacts can occur year-round but are more frequent in certain seasons. In mid-latitude areas, summer brings temperature inversions in the troposphere. These form a duct that carry VHF and UHF signals hundreds or even thousands of kilometres. Signals can remain strong for several hours or more before fading. Sporadic E also provides long-distance contacts, although it is less prevalent on 144 than 28 or 50 MHz.

FM permits the choice of simplex or repeater operation. It is less efficient than SSB but provides crisp, clear, local coverage. FM transmitters are easy to build from discrete components and more efficient class-C amplifiers can be used for RF amplification. Even milliwatts can trigger a repeater 20 or 30 km away if there are few obstructions in-between.

Then there are the orbiting repeaters, otherwise known as amateur satellites. Satellites typically transmit on one band and receive on another, for instance around 145 and 435 MHz. Some satellites may have an FM channel suitable for one contact at a time while others have linear translators that can support several simultaneous SSB/CW contacts. The easiest FM satellites, which can be readily worked with handheld transceivers and small three- or four-element yagis, are the low earth orbiting (LEO) type. LEO satellites typically allow communication within approximately a 1000 or 1500 km footprint. Conversations on satellites are kept short since passes may only last for 10 minutes before the satellite drops below the horizon and becomes unworkable. Visit amsat.org for the latest information on operating amateur satellites.

CW is not a common mode on 2 metres but has some use for weak-signal DX or auroral propagation which badly distorts SSB signals. If, after several calls, you are unsuccessful in getting your call sign across to a station you are calling on SSB, attempt a cross-mode contact by calling on CW. This may be successful if the station is a skilled VHF DXer who knows Morse.

Computer-based digital modes can span amazing distances, even with milliwatts. Conversations can be made on the faster modes (e.g. PSK-31 or JT65). The slower modes, such as WSPR, can provide confirmation that a path exists and an indication of signal strength but are most suited to unattended operation.

144 MHz provides quality local communication largely unaffected by static or varying propagation. Gain antennas are easy to build and the band is ideal for hilltop portable operating. Extended distances are possible with SSB, CW and digital modes. If you can only have one VHF/UHF band, this is it.

222 MHz (1.25 metres)

222 MHz is available in a few (mostly North American) countries. Commercially made equipment is less widely available than for other bands. Propagation characteristics include good local coverage and tropospheric enhancement during the warmer months. It is less active than 2 metres.

430 MHz (70 centimetres)

70 centimetres is a lot like 2 metres. It has a somewhat shorter communication range than 2 metres, especially in hilly areas. However, local noise on UHF can be less than VHF and signals may still be clear even if they don't indicate much on the signal strength meter. UHF coverage in cities can sometimes be better as 432 MHz tends to bounce off buildings and walls better than 144 MHz.

FM, repeater and satellite operation is similar to 2 metres. Its more localised coverage and greater number of frequencies allows use of the band for special uses such as IRLP repeaters, digital modes (e.g. P25 and DSTAR) and remote control.

VHF/UHF field-day contest rules sometimes give incentives to work 432 MHz and higher frequencies. This makes it a worthwhile band to take when portable. High-gain antennas are smaller than on 2 metres and distances of 200 km or more are readily possible with low power from a good location.

430 MHz has some interesting properties that make it worth exploring. It has many of the benefits of 144 MHz and is worth taking along when you go portable or setting up at home if you have the room.

Microwave bands

This is a specialist aspect of amateur radio. Propagation tends to be more line of sight and much activity is portable from hilltops.

Because of the difficulty and expense of generating appreciable amounts of RF power on microwave frequencies, most activity is at low power levels. The high gain of dish-style antennas allows high effective radiated power and good results. Microwaves often appeal to the technically inclined and the occasional availability of surplus, easily convertible equipment can make it both affordable and fulfilling.

Other activities

I've outlined the characteristics of the main modes and bands in use today. But how are they used and who uses them? Whether you enjoyed them in the past or wish to start second time around, below are just a few of the special interests amateurs enjoy.

VHF/UHF FM Repeaters

After World War II, the interests of technically minded amateurs swung to VHF and higher frequencies. Radar, television and the migration of land mobile communication to higher frequencies helped. As did the availability of no-code VHF/UHF-only amateur licences in many countries.

Many amateurs tried VHF AM before moving to FM and then repeaters, which were clearer than the 27 MHz AM CB then becoming popular. In this era before mobile phones, repeaters were busy and whole families often got their amateur licences.

Formerly busy 2 metre FM repeaters are quieter now, with a trend to 70 centimetres in some cities. There are more repeaters than ever before but most receive little use, even in populated areas. The old objections to holding long conversations on repeaters are no longer valid, provided adequate gaps are left between transmissions.

Nevertheless, becoming active here is still worthwhile. Most cities have at least one or two fairly busy repeaters. Equipment costs are now low, so it's only a small outlay to buy a transceiver to taste the action. As an example, cheap dual-band 2 metre/70 centimetre FM handheld transceivers are now available for under $US100 – vastly cheaper than the many hundreds of dollars charged 15 or 20 years ago. While I wouldn't recommend one as an only transceiver, their low price makes them too good to pass up.

The numerous VHF/UHF analogue FM voice repeaters that remain have been supplemented by those using various digital voice formats. Each has their advocates and a search on each will reveal varying views. Examples include:

System Fusion/C4FM (backed by Yaesu)
DMR: Digital Mobile Radio (widespread commercial use)
D-STAR: Digital Smart Technologies for Amateur Radio (backed by Icom)
P25: Project 25 (widespread commercial use)

Digital voice signals tend to be either there or not there; although audio can be distorted one never hears the harsh scratchiness of a weak analogue FM signal. Linking systems (e.g. IRLP and Echolink) often allow conversations with stations using other repeaters or even connected in via a home computer or smartphone.

Unlike the decades when everyone had FM, digital voice activity is fragmented between incompatible modes (think VHS vs Beta video formats). Digital voice transceivers are more expensive than analogue FM-only rigs and you wouldn't want to be stuck with something with no local repeaters or activity. For this reason I suggest you talk to active amateurs in your area before spending heavily on a digital voice-compatible transceiver. Another reason you want local support is that digital voice equipment requires programming and setting up, which can be daunting for the newcomer.

You can put out a CQ call on an FM simplex-calling frequency or repeater and get a response, though activity varies between areas. Again, activity has become more fragmented, spread thinly across more choices. On VHF this first came about when AM activity split into SSB for long distances and FM (often with repeaters) for local work. FM, which was initially confined to a few busy frequencies, spread wider and thinner as frequency agility became universal, thanks to phase locked loop frequency synthesisers.

More recently a similar process has been occurring with various digital voice modes competing with FM. It all gets fairly complicated, but for now I recommend starting off with a cheap FM analogue transceiver as this is the 'lingua franca' mode on the VHF/UHF bands, which nearly everyone has some capability for.

DX and contests

HF SSB and CW remain popular sub-interests that contribute to the allure of amateur radio. In many people's minds this is being able to talk near and far from your own station, independent of supporting networks or infrastructure. Those whose careers took them far from HF and analogue techniques often return to them in retirement, especially since the Morse requirement was removed.

Amateur pioneers first established the worth of HF for international communication in the 1920s. Techniques were refined and popularised. Progress was so rapid that the basic structure, procedure and culture of HF DXing, including awards and contests, were firmly established by the late 1930s.

This largely continues today, although with the inevitable changes. These include smaller and commercially made equipment, improved ease of changing bands, beacons, remote receivers, online DX spotting and electronic confirmation of contacts (QSLing). Those with the space moved from single-wire antennas to beams, while those without it moved to small verticals and loops.

At least for SSB, there appears to be less general DX activity than there used to be. The take-up of digital modes is one reason. Another is the increasing difficulty of operating in urban areas with high noise levels and shrinking yard space for antennas.

The status of DXing both within and outside amateur radio has changed. If amateur radio could once be described as 'the king of hobbies', international DXing was arguably 'the king of amateur radio'. To regularly directly talk overseas required a powerful efficient station. It was an almost magic novelty for 'the man on the street' at a time when contact with other countries and continents was rare, delayed and on other peoples' terms.

Cheap telephony, the internet and social media has democratised worldwide communication between people. Meanwhile, diversifying sub-interests within amateur radio have made it more like a mosaic than a ladder. DXing remains, but as a more specialist niche rather than its pinnacle.

Having said that, contest participation has grown and is near record highs. For those who have forgotten or never tried it, a contest is an organised event where competitors make as many contacts as possible within a defined period. This may be 24 hours for major contests, though local and more specialised contests may be over in less time. Logging is easier now, with it largely being computer- and email-based. This has contributed towards faster results that we no longer need to wait six months for.

Awards

Awards is another area that has had a renaissance. Awards are available to amateurs who have worked a sufficient number of countries, club members, geographic grid-squares, mountain summits or national parks. Think of almost any type of location you could contact and chances are someone has made an award for it.

It wasn't always thus. 30 or 40 years ago every local radio club had their own award. Work 10 or 20 members, possibly on their club net, and you'd qualify. There were also band-specific award programs such as Ten-Ten (10 metres or 28 MHz) and SMIRK (6 metres or 50 MHz). Enthusiastic amateurs could wallpaper their entire shack with certificates received.

By the 1990s, however, paper QSLing was on the wane and interest in local awards declined. Award chasing became the preserve of diehard DXers. They continued to chase the famous DXCC for working 100 or more countries, also earning endorsements for more bands, modes and countries. With rising postage and QSLing costs, the rest of us couldn't be bothered.

GETTING BACK INTO AMATEUR RADIO

Nevertheless the concept still appealed to many. All that was required was a new reason to reignite activity. Lightweight portable equipment, electronic contact confirmation (avoiding the need for slow, expensive QSLing) and email alerts provided kindling. The guilt-laced yearning of many (mainly middle-aged and pudgy) hams to 'get out more' added fuel. The conditions were then set for a new breed of awards based on outdoor portable operating.

Islands Of The Air, or IOTA, was an early one. While not everyone could fund a trip (or 'DXpedition') to an exotic DXCC country, an offshore island that qualified for IOTA was, for many amateurs, a reasonably convenient ferry ride away. You could take an HF station as hand luggage, work a stack of stations and be home by bedtime.

Potentially more strenuous is SOTA, or Summits Of The Air. Adherents get the pleasure of climbing and 'activating' mountains. Attractions include the physical challenge, the views and quiet bands free from man-made interference. SOTA has spawned a whole industry of low-power equipment and antennas suitable for the hiker. 'Summit to Summit' contacts are most sought after but working home stations (known as 'chasers') also count for award credit. Chasers who work a sufficient number of hilltop stations get the honour of being a 'SOTA Sloth'.

Taking a leaf from SOTA's book are other award programs. Particularly popular are the various national park and conservation reserve awards. Participation will take you to places not been to before. And as a sought-after station you will likely make more and better contacts than possible from home.

Minimalist radio

The 'Amateurs Code' in each ARRL Handbook extolled generations of amateurs to be progressive by operating a station that is 'well-built and abreast of science'. However, not everyone goes along with this exhortation.

There exists an alternative interest in minimalist bare-bones equipment. That is, simple one or two transistor transmitters or receivers that can be lashed together in an afternoon. As I discuss in *Minimum QRP*, they are not what you would choose to easily get contacts.

However, as a project to relearn component identification, soldering and construction skills, you could do a lot worse, especially given the low prices asked. Who, 20 or 30 years ago, thought transceiver kits would become available for the price of a hamburger? If you wish to build your own, circuits abound on the web. Start with either a simple receiver or transmitter and then later attempt a transceiver. Contacts will likely be difficult but there are numerous simple improvements that can make getting them easier.

Vintage equipment

The collection, restoration and use of historical equipment is another movement in amateur radio. The musty smell of warming dust, the heavy clunk of rotary switches and the velvet smoothness of precision tuning drives are joys of every use.

Such sensuality is absent from modern plastic-fronted, wobbly-knobbed transceivers. Old rig cabinets felt they had something in them. A kick would hurt you more than them. And etched panel markings confirmed they were built to last.

Unlike today's dainty push buttons with stunted travel and disembodied beep, toggle switches showed you where they stood. Weight, life and play made adjusting controls for nulls and peaks (as often required) both a pleasure and occasional frustration. Even if only as mechanical backlash on a bad tuning dial, it was as if the equipment was telling you something, like a ridden horse does through its reins. Not like newer gear's lack of tactility which is like a 'dead fish' handshake, all take and no give.

There are psychic as well as physical joys. The thrill of bringing neglected or dead equipment to life drives many. It's an underestimated skill. You start with nothing and almost anything done represents progress when building from scratch. Whereas with a repair it is very easy to render something that's 80% good completely useless with a careless drop or slip.

The drive to recreate a beginner station you previously owned (or wished you owned) is another reason to favour old equipment. At one time this was invariably tube gear. However 1970s analogue dial transceivers are also now starting to be referred to as 'vintage' in used-equipment ads. There are many available since a large number of people were entering amateur radio at the time and old-timers were changing from tube to solid state. Similarly, long-time 27 MHz operators cannot fail to notice often high asking prices for certain older models of CB transceiver.

My theory is that work and family responsibilities ease when people enter their 50s and 60s. Personal wealth also often peaks around then. Combined with nostalgic sentiment, made more intense as the world changes, this creates a market for products that will help relive actual or regretfully missed youth experiences. As the cohort of 60-year-olds changes, so does the era of 'peak nostalgia', which may now be entering the 1970s. If you've missed that boat, stock up on 1980s computer games and 'ghetto blasters' now!

Repairers and restorers must often draw on multiple sources for information and parts. Electronic disposals stores have all but died out and some hamfests, swap meets and radio rallies are struggling. However, the internet has transformed buying and selling by enabling a global marketplace. Those in cities may pine for the old 'Radio Row' or 'Silicon Alley' but those never near them will prefer how things are today.

We sometimes forget the unreliability of heritage equipment (or 'boat anchors'). Restored gear may need tweaking as components age and drift. Balanced modulators in sideband gear may need readjusting occasionally. And if it uses tubes (valves) it's prudent to keep a spare set. However, like children, your personal involvement in bringing something to life makes you accept quirks and forgive faults.

Competitive DXers and contesters seldom use vintage gear. But the unhurried rag chewer who rarely hops bands might. For this role performance is entirely adequate. And, provided signals are strong, the warmness of AM makes it an ideal conversational mode. Possibly most significant is that a restored or homebrew transceiver is a passport to a sub-culture in amateur radio that continues to revel in restoration, repair, tinkering and building.

As a listener you can find users of old SSB equipment scattered across the bands. Older CW or AM gear may be crystal-controlled. Listening at various times of day spread over weeks or months will likely reveal AM activity in your area. US AMers favour the top end of the 75/80 metre band, while in Australia 1825 and 7125 kHz are popular.

The last 90 years of radio history can be summarised as a move from simple to more complex modes, and from lower to higher frequencies. Radio's uses are more diverse and there has been an explosion of low-power transmitters in the hands of the public.

Amateur radio is a little different, since we are not operating under commercial constraints and our activity is drawn towards what we like, rather than what does a particular task for the least price.

7 EQUIPMENT AND TECHNOLOGY

Equipment

Amateurs continue to be inspired by waves of surplus or cheap equipment. Sixty years ago it was heavy war surplus gear. Then there was VHF AM and then FM gear as commercial users moved to higher frequencies, narrower bandwidths and trunked systems. Later we benefited from satellite or microwave cast-offs. More recently we've had the global marketplace that is eBay, and the availability of modern yet cheap equipment.

If you haven't looked at new transceiver prices lately you're in for a pleasant surprise. It's a buyers' paradise compared to 30 years ago.

Back then transceivers only covered the HF bands and cost maybe a month's wage. All-mode rigs for 50, 144 and 432 MHz were separate units and cost a similar amount each. A 160 metre to 70 cm station could have easily cost three months' pay, and we haven't even counted the accessories yet.

Today an all-mode 160 metre to 70 cm transceiver can be yours for maybe two weeks' income. And a basic 100 watt HF-only transceiver is down to a week's average wage.

VHF/UHF handheld prices have plunged even more. A 2m/70cm handheld was an expensive luxury in the 1980s and early 1990s. Today the cheapest eBay handhelds from China cost under $US50. They may lack the quality control of the established brands but their presence in the market has improved affordability for all models.

Such low prices are now seen on HF as well. At the time of writing the Bitx40 prebuilt 7 MHz SSB transceiver module is available for $US59. Solder a few wires and be on the air in an hour. The cheapest Morse transceiver kits go for under $US10 but their low output power and crystal control makes achieving contacts 'challenging', to put it politely.

Online purchasing and payment systems have further cut prices. Thirty years ago most large cities had several radio shops but are now lucky to have one. Instead, a great deal of amateur gear is available online from both domestic and overseas suppliers. Online suppliers have lower overheads and prices but you need to weigh this up against support provided by local dealers.

Warranties have lengthened on the established brands. At one time HF transceivers were guaranteed for 12 months only. Now warranties as long as five years are offered. This, coupled with lower prices, makes buying new gear more attractive than it used to be.

There remains a healthy second-hand market as amateurs upgrade to newer models. But gone are the days when each month you'd tear open a radio magazine's wrapper and head straight for the classifieds. They've almost disappeared now. Instead, keen buyers scour eBay, Facebook trading pages and various amateur-run radio sales websites. The latter sometimes offer free listings and often lower prices while eBay offers buyer protections and sometimes higher prices. Hamfests and radio club noticeboards are other sources of used transceivers and components.

Baffled by the range of transceiver models available? At one time we'd hunt down back issues of *Amateur Radio*, *Radcom* or *QST* for the review. That still happens but on a smaller scale.

Instead we go online to review websites such as eHam and QRZ. These offer greater immediacy than a monthly magazine. However, the quality of reviews varies as anyone can submit one. Still, they may give an indication of the item's age, popularity and reliability.

Thanks to YouTube, one no longer needs to know an amateur with a piece of gear to watch a demonstration. Particular brands and rigs also often have their own email lists for discussion of features and modifications.

To summarise, information on amateur equipment is much more widely available than it used to be, and it's less important to know a local expert to find it.

What about the equipment itself? For most of the past few decades the Japanese 'big three' – Icom, Yaesu and Kenwood – dominated the market as American manufacturers retreated to serve niche markets. Now the giants are under challenge and have been forced to lower their prices.

The 1980s saw three main changes to the typical amateur HF SSB transceiver. These were: tube final to solid state; analogue to digital frequency readout; and amateur band only to general coverage receivers (early 1980s advertisement below). All were available on expensive transceivers from early that decade but were standard by its end. Prices rose as the number of controls multiplied with few basic transceiver models around.

Less noisy direct digital synthesiser frequency control, digital signal processors, inbuilt power supplies and automatic antenna couplers became common during the 1990s, though often as options rather than standard. HF mobile transceivers became smaller while simultaneously covering VHF as well. And, to accommodate shrinking car dashboards, their front panels formed a detachable head unit with a cable running to the main transceiver under the seat or elsewhere.

The trend towards all-in-one transceivers accelerated in the following decade, with popular transceivers covering everything from 160 metres to 70 centimetres. The 2000s saw revived interest in small 5 or 10 watt transceivers from both established and new manufacturers. These are useful for portable operating and in countries with low-power beginner or foundation licences.

We have also seen the emergence of software defined radios. These range from simple low-power single-band kits to advanced multi-band transceivers. They may either be a box that plugs into a computer or a stand-alone transceiver with its own controls and display.

An SDR's band scope presents a frequency spectrum display. You can 'see' activity up and down the band. This is a great feature because when someone comes on either up or down the band you can see their signal. Clicking a mouse or turning a wheel lets you tune them in. SDRs sound good, deliver impressive audio and are keenly priced, especially for the receiver filtering options you get.

Another potential benefit is the additional features that come with software updates. It is, however, too early to determine whether this means we will hang on to our rigs for longer.

Transceiver kits have made a comeback. Old-timers will recall Heathkits and their step-by-step instruction manuals. Especially outside the US they were never cheap and their features were limited compared to the Japanese transceivers that dominated after about 1970.

There was a decade or two when few transceiver kits were available. The early 1990s saw somewhat of a rebirth with the growth of the QRP movement, particularly in the US. However, 1990s kits were often restricted to Morse Code on a single band.

The last 10 to 15 years have seen direct digital synthesisers that have made multi-band equipment easier to build and thus to kit. Other modes have also become available, with builders able to find kits that do SSB and/or computer-aided digital modes.

Today's kits may use through-hole and/or surface-mount parts. Kits with the latter require dexterity and suitable equipment. There are also kits which come with pre-assembled boards or modules requiring little if any soldering.

There's a happy medium when it comes to kit price and complexity. Very simple kits (e.g. the Pixie II in modified form, pictured above) cost under $US10. They are good for soldering practice but their crystal control, low transmit power and wide-open receiver makes contacts on them a challenge.

At the other end of the spectrum are expensive and more complex kits that take days, if not weeks, to assemble. Don't attempt these unless you've had recent previous experience.

I suggest starting off with a basic frequency agile SSB, DSB or CW transceiver on a popular band capable of putting out a few watts' output. Your chance of success will be higher, which will propel you onto better things if desired. Please see my e-book *Minimum QRP* for further information on suitable transceiver kits.

Perhaps the biggest change for amateur equipment has been price – and not in the direction you might expect. Unlike the 1980s, where equipment prices steadily rose, amateur equipment buyers in the 2000s paid less for gear with more bands. As an example, compare prices on the modern IC7300 with the early 1980s Yaesu FT-One in the advertisement previously shown.

The trend to lower prices shows no sign of stopping. Likely factors include cheaper materials (e.g. plastic instead of metal), the replacement of expensive parts with cheaper parts (or even software signal processing), competition from new manufacturers (eroding market share of the 'big three') and shrinking retail margins.

The information revolution and amateur radio

Those with a grandparent ham or who have been away from radio often ask if we're still around. It's a fair question given the spread of cheap and generally reliable personal communications. Yes, it's true that some who previously got into amateur radio solely for the communications aspect may see less reason to do so now.

On the other hand we've survived previous communications advances. They coexist with rather than replace the pursuit of our interest. Our stand-alone independent communications capability continues to be enjoyed and appreciated for both fun and emergency preparedness. Our high-involvement practical ethos influences and is in turn influenced by the growing hacker and maker movements.

Possibly the biggest impact of the internet is not as an alternative to amateur radio but as a facilitator of many of its activities. Just as it has changed our learning and working, the online revolution has transformed how we do radio.

The effect of online communications and commerce on equipment purchase has already been mentioned. Popular facets of amateur radio such as homebrewing, DXing, contesting, awards and QSLing are also easier now than in the past. Most of the rest of this section explains how.

Experimentation and home construction

There used to be a huge disparity in the information available to the old-timer with 30 years' worth of magazine back-issues and numerous books, and the newcomer or returning ham with nothing. Apart from the occasional lecture or overheard discussion, monthly magazines such as *Popular Electronics, Radio Electronics, Wireless World* and *Electronics Australia* were how we stayed abreast of developments.

All that has changed. Gone are the days of sitting cross-legged on the library floor hand-copying circuits from books. Instead everyone has free access to more information than they can read in a lifetime. There are circuits of almost any conceivable radio project and numerous demonstrations on YouTube.

And if you do want an extract from print, taking a photo with your smartphone can do the job in seconds. Another button press and your friends get it as well.

Parts availability has also changed. At one time the industry comprised surly middleman wholesalers who shunned small orders of specialist parts from people without trade accounts. We were instead supposed to buy from local retailers who rarely stocked many RF components. These outlets had the market to themselves as foreign ordering was too hard for most.

We've since seen the departure of both chain and independent shops from the specialist radio and enthusiast market. Their loyal but small band of customers was insufficient for owners who dropped the small parts, built more and bigger stores and chased the already-competitive consumer market. These strategies proved a failure and within a few years formerly massive chains were gone.

There are still some 'bricks and mortar' component stores (e.g. Maplin in the UK and Jaycar in Australia) but they are a long trip for many. However, previously trade-only outlets opened to the general public while a host of local and international online suppliers cater for more specialised items. Their prices are often attractive, and individual parts can be shipped here for less than local postage alone could cost.

With a worldwide electronic marketplace, even valves, tuning capacitors and crystals are probably easier to get than in the 1990s, though beware of paying inflated 'vintage' prices. Test gear has also become more available. Direct-reading inductance and capacitance meters are common, and antenna analysers have largely replaced the old noise bridge and dip oscillator.

The 1960s home-brewing hams often got their start with a Geloso VFO for their communications receiver or transmitter. Then followed several decades where anyone who wanted to generate a stable RF signal were on their own. Direct digital synthesiser modules and kits offering excellent frequency range and stability have become available in the past decade or so. DDS modules have made the concept of ordinary amateurs building multi-band HF transceivers less far-fetched than 30 years ago.

Those not wishing to build a transceiver from scratch but want the assurance of a proven circuit might try a kit. There are more HF transceiver kits available now than 40 years ago. They range from those using largely salvaged or discrete parts (such as the BitX SSB transceiver) to designs incorporating programmable electronics such as Arduino micro-controllers and software defined signal processing.

Online forums, email lists and Facebook pages have brought adherents of a particular interest closer together, although there aren't as many specialist VHF groups as there were years ago. Even so, social media provides a more efficient way to arrange tests than calling on an obscure unmonitored band or individually phoning those with known capability.

Antennas

No matter how much technology makes our equipment smaller and cheaper, the old rule of antenna design remain unchanged: there is no such thing as a free lunch. Antennas claiming wide no-tune bandwidth, high efficiency and small size are illusions. One can have two of these but never three.

That's not to say that there haven't been changes. These have come about through greater access to and influence of antenna modelling software, smaller blocks and renewed interest in portable operating. Off-centre dipoles and easy-to-erect end-fed antennas seem to have become more popular, especially for portable operating.

Another change has been in how we support our antennas. Fishing outlets sell lightweight telescopic 8 or 9 metre squid poles for about $US50. Compacting down to barely a metre, they make perfect masts for portable or temporary home operating. While flexible at the top, they are still strong enough to support a variety of thin-wire vee and vertical antennas.

Automatic antenna couplers offer fast band change without knob twiddling. They're even available in rugged outdoor versions, making it possible to position them at the antenna rather than transceiver end. This allows easier and more efficient multi-band operation from random-length wire antennas.

Undergrounding of power lines, the switch to digital TV and the decline of 27 MHz activity made vertical structures in the suburbs fewer and smaller. The amateur antenna thus sticks out more than it used to. Unit complexes may ban them altogether. Popular responses that test our ingenuity include concealed or disguised antennas, temporary masts, use of high-efficiency digital modes or portable operating. Further ideas for antennas are presented in the next chapter.

DXing

Once upon a time one only knew of propagation conditions and DX activity through prediction charts in monthly magazines and listening on one's only radio. Since then real-time observations have largely replaced predictions. This is exemplified by online DX clusters and social media, which have narrowed the gap between the first and last to know. This has resulted in intense pile-ups of wanted stations as soon as word gets around.

Equally revolutionary is that it is no longer even necessary to work someone to get an idea of where and how strong your signal is. CW operators have the <u>Reverse Beacon</u> website, comprising a worldwide network or remote receivers and CW decoders whose outputs are aggregated and displayed at near real-time on the web. Call CQ on any HF band and chances are some RBN station will list you.

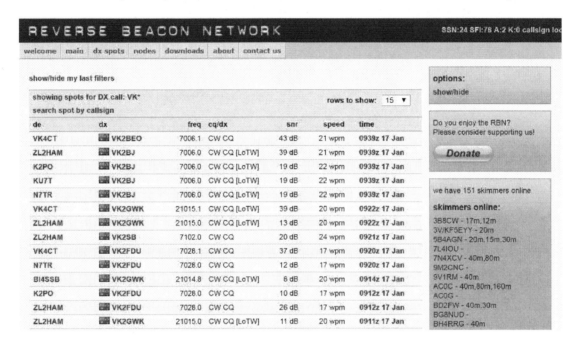

SSB operators don't quite have this level of automation available. However, they can dial up a web receiver and hear the strength of their voice coming back from a remote location.

These developments have meant that we're operating with much more information in real-time than we did in the past, including an ability to receive and compare our own signals from a remote receiver.

QSLing, awards and contests

Paper QSLing has always been expensive and laborious. We enjoyed the colourful card from overseas but cursed filling out hundreds of cards from a DXpedition long after our suntans had worn off. Bureaux still exist for those who wish to use them. However, faster alternatives to QSLing are gaining ground and saving hams money. These include eQSL and the ARRL's Logbook of the World.

Operating awards used to involve gathering QSLs and forwarding proof of contacts to the Award Manager. Radio organisations such as Australia's WIA have developed slick online methods that have made applying easier. Interest in awards has been revived and there are now more applications. In addition, popular new awards such as Summits on the Air have rejuvenated portable and hilltop operating around the world.

Ever entered a contest and waited months for the results to appear? Paper logs, contest managers' workloads and magazine deadlines were major contributing factors. Now electronic logging and online submission have become common. The result is that more entrants are emailing their logs from just after the contest has finished. Sooner arrival and computerised logs are allowing better cross-checking and earlier publication of results.

8 ANTENNAS AND STATION SETUP

Antennas are the only publicly visible portion of an amateur station and, as mentioned before, can cause difficulties with landlords, local councils, bodies corporate and home owner associations. City councils may have planning rules with height limits. Property titles and lease agreements can be even more restrictive, with fine print that prohibits any outdoor antenna. This is particularly the case in areas where underground power and cable television mean an amateur's antenna is much more visible than in the past.

Prevention is better than cure. If moving house check that wherever you are moving to has a clear title with no restrictive covenants. Such titles are more common in established neighbourhoods than newer master-planned communities with a home-owners association or body corporate. Restrictions are also likely to be less for a separate house than an apartment, unit or condominium.

Having said that, small groups of units or row houses may have no common property and no active body corporate, so you may be in luck there as well. Of course, such smaller dwellings have less space for antennas as well as closer neighbours so they are generally less attractive for radio. But there are typically buying criteria other than radio, such as location and price, and we often have to make do.

Rental tenants have their own problems, although there is the consolation that moving out is easier than for home owners. Circumstances in other countries may vary, but at least here in Australia most landlords have a real estate agent or property manager collect rent and perform periodic inspections. The average manager is very busy and may look after 100 or more properties. It is rare for them to spend more than five or ten minutes inside your home when doing the inspection. Chances are they won't even enter the back yard unless there is something about your tenancy that causes them to inspect more thoroughly.

What can you do if you aren't planning to move house but wish to set up an antenna or two? The first thing is to be aware of where any opposition may come from.

For instance, local councils may have planning ordinances that include height limits in residential areas. A thin pole holding up a VHF/UHF vertical or HF wire antenna will probably go unnoticed. Something like a tower with HF beam may require a building permit. More substantial structures may also require a planning permit, which can be quite an involved process.

Closer to home I've already mentioned the possibility of objection from homeowner associations or bodies corporate. Despite what the fine print says, you might be able to get away with modest antennas if you have good relationships with neighbours and you're a volunteer with the homeowner association (e.g. an onsite rep or president).

Opposition might come from an even closer quarter if your spouse or others at home do not share your reignited enthusiasm for radio.

Luckily there are ways around most of these objections and situations. With any luck the returning ham will be able to find a way to erect two or three inconspicuous, modest but useful outdoor antennas without needing to apply to any authority for permission.

Because circumstances vary so much by region, there's no substitute for local advice. Talking to hams in your area is a good bet. Almost everyone at your local radio club will have antennas at home. They will be only too happy to share good and bad experiences. Alternatively, when mobile you could raise the topic on VHF/UHF repeaters or even knock on the doors of nearby homes you notice with large antennas.

Contrary to pictures on QSL cards or in magazines, only a few amateurs own large land holdings. Most of us need to be creative with the type and location of antennas we erect. Being able to see antenna opportunities even in difficult locations is one of the most important (and satisfying) skills any ham can learn (or relearn). Be inspired by the following who have found solutions to their antenna problems.

The patriot

Some, especially in the US, proclaim their civic pride by flying a flag. Flagpoles may be more accepted than antenna masts in some areas. Why not have the flagpole do double duty? Many hams find that flagpoles make great covers for vertical antennas or supports for wires.

The concealer

Those with big trees in their yard can use it to hide a strategically placed pole. Or they can use its branches to support an entire antenna. Tree-concealed quad and delta loops perform well and, if fed with open wire feedline, can work on several bands. The same goes for ground planes or verticals on VHF.

A careful choice of wire, feedline, masts, baluns and supports can help the antenna blend in and be all but invisible to all but those who know it's there.

The roof improviser

Most people going about their daily duties do not look up at the roof. Which is just as well, since roofs have many things that can be antenna supports or tie-off points.

Chimneys with TV antennas are one. If you don't have a TV antenna, why not put one up even if all your TV is cable or satellite? Or you might have developed an interest in FM radio listening, which for maximum distance will need a small beam antenna. Leave it up for a few months and see if anyone objects. If anyone does, it can be replaced with something smaller, which could (very conveniently) be beams for 144 MHz and/or 432 MHz.

Toilets often have vent pipes poking through the roof. A couple of U-bolts can hold a vertical for VHF and/or UHF. If made with PVC tubing painted the same colour as the pipe, no one will notice its addition.

Monoband coax-fed and multi-band open-wire fed dipole antennas do not use traps or loading coils. Thus they can use thin wire that is almost invisible at more than a few metres' distance. Also, only lightweight insulators and supports are needed. These can be cheap everyday items such as offcuts from plastic kitchen chopping boards (for insulators) and fishing line (for support lines).

The antenna should be as far as possible from roofing. About 50 cm should be sufficient for tiles but those with an iron roof will want greater distance. You may need to be ingenious with how you hold the antenna away. Chimneys, gutters and trees can be helpful tie-off points. Others use a small tripod as a stand-off. Even if you have to zig-zag a dipole to suit available space or mounting points, you'll find its performance better than almost any other 'stealth' or compact antenna.

Metal roofs can be both friend and foe. They are a nuisance if using attic antennas or near horizontal wires, but they can form excellent ground planes for vertical antennas. Even if your house has tiles maybe there is a shed or carport with a metal roof you can use. If you're worried about the height and visibility of vertical antennas, consider the potential of telescopic rods.

The telescoper

Ever dreamt about a 12 to 17 metre mast but resigned yourself to not having one due to a small yard and close-at-hand neighbours? Sure, building one out of timber or metal is a significant engineering feat and might stick out like a sore thumb. But what about a temporary structure that's only up in the early mornings or at night when you're on air?

Lightweight fibreglass telescoping poles that collapse down to a metre are now readily available for less than you might think. They won't support an HF beam but will hold most other antennas, including verticals, dipoles, quads, loops and more. The cheaper 7 to 9 metre models, available from fishing equipment suppliers, suffice for temporary or portable operating with light wire antennas.

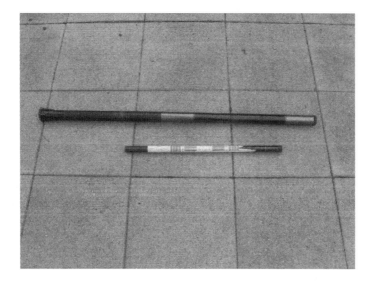

More expensive types, such as the Spiderbeam poles, are heavier, thicker and stronger. A 12 metre pole can be handled by one person and represents a good compromise between price, height and ease of handling. If you're really keen, 17 metre types are also available. They are harder to handle, not cheap but allow 'big station' performance. Choose these for semi-permanent operation from home or if you need to support heavier antennas.

Such temporary structures are much less likely to raise the ire of council and neighbours. Their short erection time is a small price to pay for their good on-air results.

Those in the tropics have other options. Bamboo is an outstandingly light and strong support for wire antennas. It may be available for the taking in some areas. If you have a long narrow yard, you may be able to make a tilting system so the antenna is below fence height whenever you are not operating.

The balcony broadcaster

Imagine how good it would be to live atop a tower. You'd enjoy the height, there'd be no need to climb it and cable runs would be short, lessening losses. Some of these benefits accrue to those in high-rise apartments with balconies.

If a balcony is wide enough for a bicycle it's wide enough for a magnetic loop. Available to buy or easy to build at home, a single loop can support operation on most HF bands.

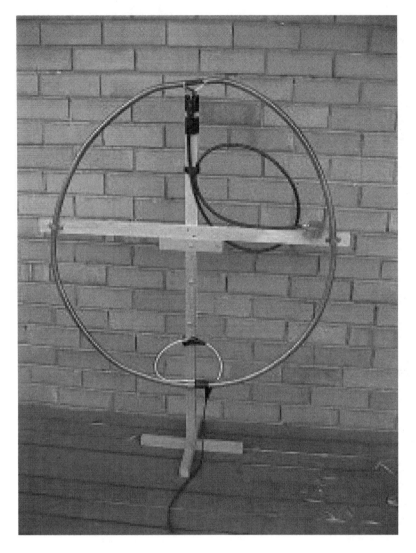

Could a washing line do double duty as an antenna on a band like 6 or 10 metres? Alternatively you may choose to dangle a wire, possibly using a telescoping pole to stand it off from the building. A good antenna coupler allows multi-band operation. On VHF/UHF a set of yagis can radiate a formidable signal in the direction your balcony faces. Hills can be a blessing as you can beam towards them and bounce signals in the opposite direction.

The attic crawler

If you've got a non-metal roof and a means to access inside it, then the attic or roof cavity can be a handy place to string an antenna. Depending on the size of your roof space, you may be able to erect HF dipoles, small loops or VHF/UHF verticals. Access to the roof space is typically from the inside via a trap door or from outside by removing a few tiles. Expect higher interference on receive compared to an 'in the clear' antenna but results should still be better than an indoor antenna.

The eavesdropper

Houses with timber eaves can be useful for the experimenter who wishes to keep their antenna invisible below roof height. Fine wire pinned to the eaves can form an antenna, though you'd want to exhaust most other antenna options before going down this road. You wouldn't want to run more than a few watts, receive noise will be high and transmit performance won't be good. Still, you should still get out, especially if using weak signal digital modes.

The gutter loader

Some regard gutters around the roof as a ready-made antenna. A good antenna coupler connected to one can load it up on a variety of HF frequencies. Like a wire around the eaves, it is likely to pick up noise from house wiring and appliances. Another thing to watch for is the risk of corroded connections rectifying your transmitted signal and radiating harmonics. This can be hard to trace. For this reason I regard roof gutters as a last-resort antenna option.

The mobileer

A variant of the temporary antenna is one affixed to a vehicle. Regular mobile antennas aren't the most efficient but other options exist. For example, ingenious amateurs have devised mounting plates that when parked on form a stable mount for a collapsible mast. Another option is a trailer-mounted pneumatic mast. A wire can be run to this from inside your house, or, even better, the whole station driven to a good RF spot.

The wanderer

Some are lucky to live in the hills or beside a river, bay or ocean. Or maybe there is a park a short distance away. A location even a hundred metres from houses is likely to be much quieter for HF receiving than one surrounded by them. Salt water can assist signals on HF while on VHF/UHF a clear outlook is an advantage.

If you have such nearby geographic advantages, you may not invest in a station at home but instead devote your effort to one that can be taken afield at a moment's notice. It could either be carried by vehicle, hand-pulled shopping trolley or backpack. As well as the location benefits, the novelty value of such portable operation should increase the number of contacts made. This is not least due to the number of operating activities and events created for special locations such as mountain summits or national parks.

Below is a low-power HF station small enough to be carried to a park or beach. Everything fits inside the blue case, which in turn fits inside a small backpack. Key items include battery, transceiver, antenna coupler and telescoping pole for the antenna.

More of a challenge (but a novelty for the stations worked) is HF operating while walking. A portable vertical or magnetic loop (pictured below) are my favourite antennas. Contacts within one's own continent are possible on 7 MHz while 14 MHz and higher can work for worldwide communications, even with low transmitter output powers. My website vk3ye.com has further articles and videos on HF pedestrian mobile.

Seven questions to ask

I've given some ideas as to how amateurs get around the antenna challenges presented by their location. It is worth using your imagination to see how they apply to your location and circumstances.

Asking the following questions might help get you thinking:

1. Do you have a backyard, courtyard or balcony?

2. Are there trees that could support a wire or pole?

3. Is there a long narrow space beside the house that could accommodate a tilt-over mast?

4. Is there a high upstairs window you could use to stick something out of?

5. Can you get access to the roof either through an internal trap door or from outside?

6. Are there things on or near the roof that could support a wire, mast or stand-off, such as a chimney, TV antenna, toilet vent pipe or overhanging tree?

7. Is there a ready-made means of getting a wire from inside to outside (or to the roof space) e.g. a disused chimney, vent or window?

No doubt other possibilities will reveal themselves. Even when a location appears at first sight hopeless for radio, my experience is that it is usually possible to do some form of transmitting activity.

The antenna itself

As for the antenna type itself, a simple vertical or ground plane for VHF/UHF FM and dipoles for a couple of popular HF bands are good starting points. There are abundant ideas on the web and detailed discussion in the *Minimum QRP* and *Hand-carried QRP antennas* ebooks.

To get you started, here's some common lossy or ineffective antennas I suggest avoiding:

- **Coax-fed dipole with an antenna coupler near the transceiver for other bands**

A coax fed dipole (or vertical) works well on its design band but is not so good elsewhere. That's even if an antenna coupler is used. While this can be adjusted so a 1:1 SWR is indicated and the transmitter delivers its full rated output, losses multiply due to mismatches at the antenna end and resultant increased feedline losses.

- **Dipoles shorter than 3/8 wavelength at the lowest operating frequency**

You can shorten a dipole by about a quarter and it will still be okay if fed with open wire feedline. However, losses mount when it is made much shorter, for instance trying to load a 40 metre dipole up on 80 metres.

- **Short verticals with poor ground systems**

Short verticals, often with traps, appeal if you can't achieve much height. Trapped antennas can be reasonably efficient if a narrow bandwidth is accepted. However, this takes a lot of time cutting and testing every time the antenna is installed at a new location. An antenna coupler can allow the transceiver to deliver its full output power but additional feedline losses will still occur.

- **Quarter-wave end-feds with poor ground systems**

Possibly the simplest HF antenna is a quarter wavelength of wire with one end stuck into the transceiver's antenna socket and the other run to a tree or pole. This can work for a quick test on 80 metres but losses are similar to a short vertical without a good ground. Performance only becomes satisfactory if you can clip on to a good ground such as a metal fence or pier.

- **Anything that claims small size, wide bandwidth <u>and</u> high efficiency**

You can save space with loading coils on dipoles and verticals. Small magnetic loops can also give good results. But only if their bandwidth is narrow. The golden rule of compact antennas is that unless the bandwidth is narrow it won't be efficient; anything that claims otherwise is a con.

- **Antennas with unsuitable radiation patterns**

Different antennas have different angles of radiation that affect your signal strength at the other end. An otherwise efficient antenna may fail if it radiates mostly to the wrong places.

As an example, a vertical for the lower HF bands is good for short groundwave contacts and low-angle DX but not so good for intermediate distances that rely on high-angle propagation.

Conversely, a low horizontal dipole is poor for local groundwave contacts on 160 metres. Even a short vertical would be better. But the dipole might be better for evening sky wave contacts at distances just beyond where the groundwave signal finishes.

Big stations have several switchable antennas for each band. Portable stations may only carry a couple of antennas with only one up at a time. Your selection should be optimised for the most common contacts on each band, for instance up to several hundred kilometres on the lower HF bands and 1000 km or more on the higher HF bands.

Be aware that cost and antenna performance are not necessarily related. There are expensive commercially made antennas that are a significant performance compromise. Conversely, you can get good results from a simple wire. Ignore manufacturers' claims unless they are verified by independent reviews.

9 PROPAGATION

The characteristics of various bands were discussed briefly earlier. Each HF band has different propagation characteristics to those above and below. Bands fall into two main groups, above and below about 10 MHz.

- Below 10 MHz

HF frequencies below 10 MHz are open for the longest distances at night, and also around dawn and dusk. 1.8 and 3.5 MHz support short range communications during the day while 7 and 10 MHz allow daytime coverage up to about 1000 km. The daytime difference is due to the high absorption of 1.8 and often 3.5 MHz signals in the ionosphere's D layer and generally high urban noise levels. These two factors mask signals and are the reason that the 1.8 and 3.5 MHz bands appear dead during the day. 5 and 7 MHz frequencies have less absorption and noise so are more effective for the daytime QRPer.

7 and 10 MHz operators especially need to be aware of the critical frequency – the absorption limiting frequency (ALF) or lowest usable frequency (LUF) – and its effect on propagation. The critical frequency is defined as the highest frequency at which a signal radiated straight up will return to its origin. Frequencies below the critical frequency will provide a blanket-like coverage while those above will first return to earth some hundreds of kilometres from the transmitter, skipping over intermediate areas. Like the maximum usable frequency, the critical frequency tends to be higher during the day and when there is higher solar activity. You can find the F2 critical frequency on propagation websites such as ips.gov.au.

The daytime critical frequency can vary from well below 7 MHz to above 10 MHz, depending on solar activity. A low critical frequency typical during low sunspot years makes 7 MHz volatile for communication between about 50 and 300 km but good for around 800 km. 7 MHz becomes highly reliable between 0 and about 700 km during intermediate sunspot years. Because 10 MHz is still above the typical critical frequency, the band is much less reliable than 7 MHz for short distances but superior for daytime communication above about 800 km. More sunspots allow 10 MHz to cover shorter distances (by supporting higher radiation angles) and reduce the maximum distances possible on 7 MHz (due to higher absorption).

The critical frequency drops greatly at night whatever the phase of the solar cycle. This brings it closer to lower HF frequencies such as 1.8, 3.5 and 5 MHz. This is why these bands come alive at night with contacts possible up to thousands of kilometres, even sometimes with QRP. Night critical frequencies always exceed 1.8 MHz and nearly always 3.5 MHz. It is this characteristic that allows these bands to provide blanket skywave coverage, even including intermediate distances where the daytime groundwave signal has petered out. Just like with 7 MHz during the day, low sunspot numbers can play havoc with 3.5 MHz at night, with depressed critical frequencies making usually strong 100 to 300 km distance signals weak and watery. A bonus, though, is that in areas with high close-in amateur populations local QRM is less and you may have more readable signals from DX stations. This may increase opportunities to make long-distance two-way QRP contacts on the lower HF bands.

- Above 10 MHz

Above 10 MHz are the 'daytime bands'. Worldwide communication occurs most often during the day, especially within a few hours of dawn and dusk. Night-time activity is much less, especially during low sunspot years. Because these bands are nearly always above the 'critical frequency', signals on them are seldom reflected to locations near the transmitting station, except on days when solar activity is very high. Consequently the higher HF bands only occasionally support communication in the 50 to 500km range and high-angle radiation from antennas is lost into space.

The most important frequency to be aware of when exploring the higher HF bands is the 'maximum usable frequency' or MUF. The MUF tends to be higher when high sunspot numbers cause heightened ionisation of the ionosphere. It is not a fixed number but is dependent on the propagation path and time of day. For example, north-south paths that cross the equator have a higher MUF than east-west contacts, especially where signals pass near the polar regions. Also, like the critical frequency discussed before, the MUF is higher during the day and lower at night. Propagation websites can give you current MUFs.

The optimum working frequency for a path is sometimes considered to be about 80% of its MUF as losses are still low.

Related to this is the common adage that low power operators should operate on the highest frequency band that is open. I am not so convinced about this. There are many times when weak signals are audible on bands like 24 or 28 MHz but no one is workable. You may have more success on a lower band, such as 14 MHz, that is fully open and has stronger signals. Experimenters testing long-distance antipodean paths such as Europe to Australia or New Zealand have found that middle HF frequencies providing greater reliability, possibly due to more efficient 'chordal hop' propagation within the ionosphere. A great deal of data to test best frequencies for particular paths can be gathered by transmitting and receiving WSPR signals on various bands.

One way to visualise HF propagation on various frequencies at various times is to imagine you are frying an egg in a pan. Picture the pan is the whole world on which a great circle map (an azimuthal equidistant projection) centred on your station has been printed. An example map, centred on Florida, is shown below. Visit ns6t.net to generate one for your location.

Azimuthal Map
Center: 28°6'54"N 80°37'54"W
Courtesy of Tom (NS6T)

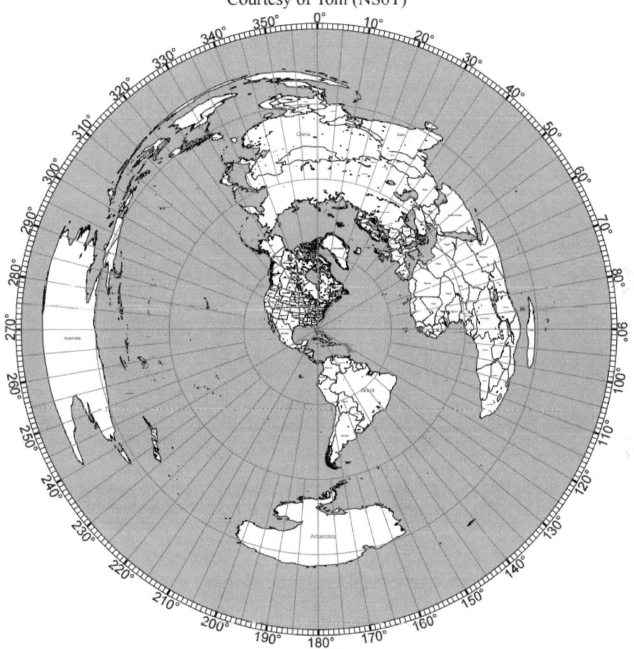

The yolk in the 'fried egg' diagrams below is the area of groundwave propagation. Its radius is proportional to wavelength. In other words, lower frequencies have a longer groundwave range. If applying the pan analogy to the upper HF or VHF, we could also use the yolk to represent close-in direct or 'line of sight' coverage.

The white represents the skywave coverage area. Its coverage of the pan is affected by factors like frequency, time of day and solar activity. The white may be thick, thin or not form at all. Other times it may be uneven, as if the pan has been tilted, to extend further in some directions than others. Or it may separate from the yolk exposing a ring of the pan not covered. In RF parlance that represents a skip zone, i.e. an area beyond groundwave coverage but too close for the signals on a particular frequency to return to earth.

Consider each band, time and solar activity combination as a different type of egg which behaves differently in the pan.

Some examples are below. Low HF represents approximately 1.8 to 3.5 MHz, medium HF represents 5 to 10 MHz and upper HF represents 14 MHz and above.

Low solar activity

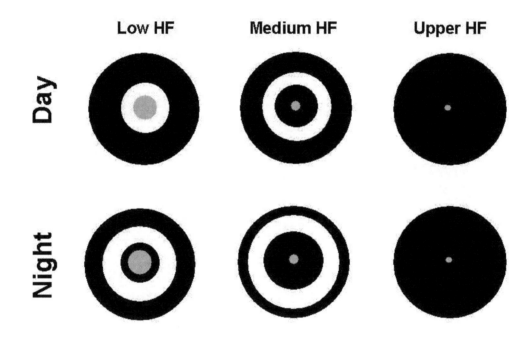

Moderate solar activity

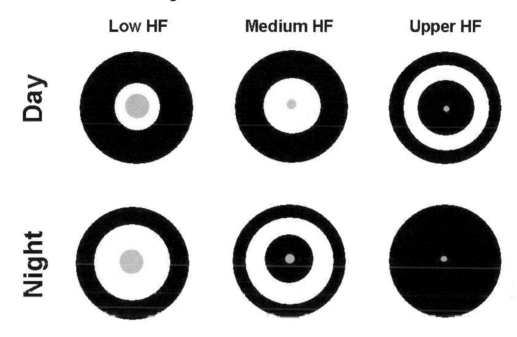

High solar activity

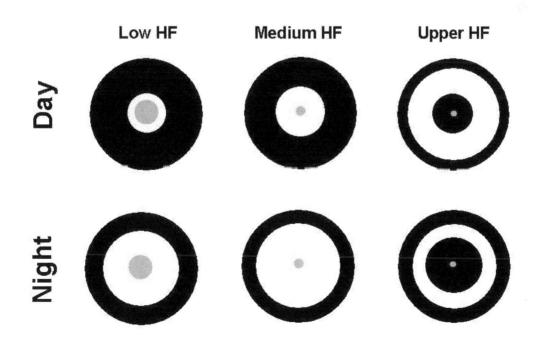

Comparing these charts to what you hear on the bands can be instructive. You'll first notice day and night variation by frequency. Also, if you've got a good memory of your previous operating, you'll remember variations attributable to solar activity. For example, 7 MHz allows blanket coverage during high sunspot years but skips over certain distances when solar activity is low. On the other hand, distances of about 1000 km during the day propagate better during the lower sunspot years as absorption is lower, being nearer the MUF. While most hams yearn for the solar peaks, it's also important to be aware of and exploit the opportunities that solar troughs allow.

- Above 28 MHz

Amateurs active from the late 1940s to the early 2000s benefited from an unusual number of above-average sunspot peaks. They enjoyed outstanding long-distance contacts on 28 and 50 MHz and there was only one cycle, in the late 1960s, that was not particularly strong.

The peak just gone (2012 to 2014) was low by recent historical standards. Current expert thinking at the time of writing is that future peaks will also be weak. Pessimists sometimes even raise the possibility of another Maunder Minimum, where sunspot numbers stayed depressed for decades.

Today's amateurs may have to change their expectations of working long distances on 28 and 50 MHz. The good news, though, is that these bands will continue to provide 1000 to 3000 km contacts independent of sunspot numbers, thanks to Sporadic E propagation.

This is most common for a few weeks around mid-summer (and a little in winter). It can occur at any time but is most likely from late morning. Sporadic E is a fun but volatile mode and the places you'll be able to work will vary during an opening. The strong signals involved make summer operating on 28 and 50 metres highly rewarding, even with simple antennas such as a low ground plane, dipole or delta loop. Sporadic E also occurs on 144 MHz but is much less common.

- Above 144 MHz

Higher VHF, UHF and microwave signals are not influenced by sunspots but can be propagated long distances if there is a tropospheric inversion. Inversions can form a low-loss duct able to carry signals over several hundred to a few thousand kilometres. Distant beacons become audible while you may be able to trigger several repeaters on the one frequency. This is unwelcome for commercial users due to the risk of interference but gives amateurs variety in what they can work on the VHF and UHF bands.

Inversions are most likely during the summer months but can occur any time of the year. Best times are often around sunrise and sunset, with peak condition lasting for a few hours. Over-water paths are especially favoured. Extreme antenna height on hilltops can sometimes be a hindrance if it means signals are projected above the duct zone.

I've covered the main modes of propagation likely to be useful on various bands. Despite being on the downslope of a solar cycle, distant communication will still be possible. The difference is that more of it will be worked below 14 or 18 MHz. The higher HF and VHF/UHF bands will still have their moments, particularly at times when Sporadic E propagation or tropospheric ducting is intense.

IO GETTING CONTACTS

Some amateurs report having difficulty making contacts, especially if running low power or their licence category imposes substantial mode and frequency restrictions (e.g. the US Technician class on HF). This section discusses approaches to getting on-air contacts. I'll start with HF and discuss VHF/UHF later.

Active bands easiest to get a contact during the day include 20 or 40 metres. At night, 80 or 40 metres are often good choices. Choose bands either side if crowding is acute as these will often be open.

Roughly survey conditions and activity by quickly scanning several bands each time you turn on. This familiarises you with activity patterns and propagation.

Do another pass once you've settled on a band that deserves more attention. Tune slowly, stop on all stations (even the weaker ones) and listen actively. Note call signs and approximate station locations to gauge conditions.

Memorise or write down the frequencies of stations you think will soon sign off or resume calling CQ. These will be useful for reasons explained later. Conversely, less attention should be paid to (i) long-winded contacts on topics not of interest, (ii) contacts in modes (or languages) you can't understand and (iii) stations calling exclusively for a particular station, activity or contest.

The four main approaches to getting HF contacts are:

- Replying to stations calling CQ
- Calling stations that have just finished a contact ('tail-ending')
- Calling CQ
- Breaking in on an existing contact

Replying to stations calling CQ

This is perhaps the easiest way of getting contacts, especially if running low power and the station calling is not 'rare DX'. Slowly tune the band listening for stations calling CQ. When you find one, listen until you've heard their call sign clearly. Then reply one or two seconds after they finish.

When calling, announce their call sign followed by yours. Since they will likely be unfamiliar with it, your pronunciation should be clear, slow and preferably repeated. Use phonetics if signals are likely to be weak or the pace of operating is slow. If things are fast-moving, such as during a contest, announce your call sign only.

The calling station may return to you, another station, a station they did not properly hear or no one.

If they return to another station, keep listening. They (or the other station) may have heard you and call you in. Or it may be a short contact and there is a chance to try again soon if they resume calling.
There will be times when the calling station knows that someone is calling but hasn't heard them strong enough to discern the call sign. They will then reply 'QRZ' or 'call again'. Give your call again but more slowly, clearly and in proper phonetics.

If the calling station replies to no one, give them a second call. Otherwise keep listening in case they resume their calling. If they get no answers and you are unsuccessful after several tries, note their signal strength but give them a miss for now. Later on, if they are still calling and conditions improve, you may stand a better chance.

Once contact has been established, exchange basic details like signal reports, names and locations. Fast DX or contest contacts may not get this far while more leisurely contacts can continue as long as desired.

There are other tricks. If you hear a carrier signal varying in strength or someone announce that they are testing, keep listening. They may just be checking their station before calling CQ. If you're there for their first call you may be the first they work.

Some stations issue directional calls, for instance a particular prefix, country or just plain "CQ DX". Respect these wishes and do not call the station if you do not fall within the prefix or area sought.

A partial exception to the above is if you hear a station making many calls without replies. Newcomers running low power especially may spend ages fruitlessly calling "CQ DX" despite their output power and band condition not being conducive to long-distance contacts. In this case they may appreciate a call from you.

Replying to others' CQ calls is a highly successful way of getting contacts. However, there are times when the band is active but no one is calling CQ. Here's where you need to apply other methods.

"Tail-ending" contacts that have just finished

As well as searching for stations calling CQ, another part of 'active listening' is keeping tabs on contacts about to finish. Established contacts can decline when no new topics are raised or conversation goes around in circles. When one person leaves a group of three or four often those remaining sign off shortly after. Time listening will let you relearn such cues.

This is important because after stations sign there is often someone listening, whether a party to the original contact or someone else 'on the side'. When someone is there, tuned up and listening, you are more likely to get a contact than if calling on a random 'cold' frequency.

Tail-ending is simply calling one of those who were previously there. Call the strongest first since they are more likely to hear you, especially if you aren't running much power. Sometimes those on the frequency may have switched off but a listening station will, after an interval, call and a contact will ensue.

Never talk over people; only call when a frequency's occupants have all truly signed. Judgement is required since some stations do not cleanly sign or may return with 'final-finals'. This will come with practice as you get to know the voices and operating habits of band regulars.

'Tail-ending' is a highly successful approach to contact-getting. Like answering others' CQ calls, it requires active listening. This is an art that any newcomer and returnee to amateur radio would do well to practice.

Calling CQ

If there are no contacts about to end or stations calling CQ, the next approach is to create your own activity by calling CQ. First find a clear frequency. On SSB this should be at least three and preferably five kilohertz away from the nearest occupied frequency. For Morse on a quiet band, position yourself at least two or three kilohertz away as not everyone has narrow filters. If it's really busy, such as during a major contest, you can crowd in closer, e.g. several hundred hertz to one kilohertz. Listen a bit more and then ask if the frequency is in use ('QRL?' on CW).

Then call CQ with your call sign clearly announced and repeated. The length of your call depends on band activity. Make it shorter if the band is very active and longer if it is quiet. Leave sufficient time for listening and resume calling if no replies.

Be patient. Don't give up if no one replies. Instead, quickly tune the band looking for others calling CQ or for contacts about to finish. If you find nothing, return to calling. Listeners are turning on and tuning across the band at any time and you may call for 15 minutes or more before you get a reply.

Computers, digital voice recorders, timers and micro-controllers can all be connected to a transceiver to automatically call CQ. Some post on social media to say they are calling CQ. These strategies are perfectly legal though in some minds such methods detract from the joy of receiving a spontaneous reply from someone randomly tuning past.

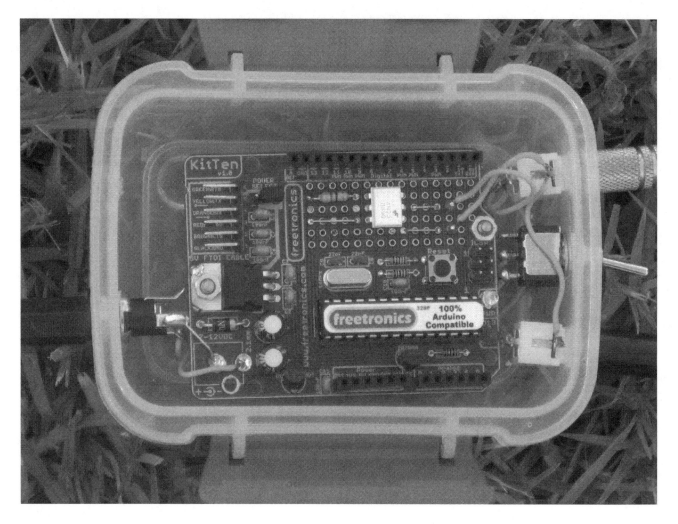

Calling CQ doesn't work for everyone. If you are running low power or a compromise antenna, your signal may be weak or inaudible. As most generally reply to strong, readable signals, you may not get many contacts. Crowded, DX-oriented or spasmodically open bands such as 14 to 30 MHz can sometimes be difficult to get replies on.

While a test of perseverance, calling CQ is a rewarding way of making contacts. Success here demonstrates your antenna and station are effective, which should be the aim of every amateur.

Breaking in on contacts

If there are no stations calling CQ, no contacts about to end and no replies to persistent CQ calls, another way to get contacts is to break in to a conversation already in progress.

Breaking in is arguably the least 'sporting' way to make contacts. Certain conversations are best left alone, such as those on a detailed topic to which you cannot contribute. Also avoid breaking in on contacts where you can't hear everyone since some probably won't hear you. This becomes a mess with endless repetitions and relays. Instead, wait for the group to finish and 'tail-end' call a station you can hear.

All my most enjoyable contacts have involved four or fewer stations. Above that the quality of conversation declines as depth drops and more time is spent on working out who goes next. If a group is already large, resist the temptation to break in until a few have signed. This keeps numbers manageable and the conversation flowing.

In other cases breaking in may be appropriate. Examples include where you can contribute or answer a question posed. And a station testing their equipment may welcome signal or audio reports.

Timing is the golden rule when breaking in. This comes with practice. Clearly announce your call sign in the break between transmissions – never transmit over another station. Also, unless it an emergency never say 'break' or 'break break'. The main exception is if you are already in the conversation and wish to quickly interrupt the order of proceedings to pass a quick message.

With any luck you will be acknowledged and called in. This may be almost immediately or after everyone has had their next turn. Keep listening even if you aren't acknowledged; there may be others who did hear you and will call you in later.

The first transmission when invited to speak should be short. It should comprise your name, location, signal reports for other stations and why you broke in. Later transmissions can be longer, depending on conversation flow.

Reasons for you not being acknowledged vary. They include you not being heard. The stations you are breaking in to may be in animated discussion. If they were not expecting others they may have set their receiver's gain low or left only short gaps between transmissions. If you're not successful after a couple of tries, note their frequency and search instead for other stations that may be easier to work.

The operating culture on VHF and UHF FM is a little different to HF as the generally local coverage means it is the same people talking day in and day out. Some FM repeater users announce that they are 'listening'. Treat this like a CQ call and reply accordingly if you are within range. Otherwise, the above approaches to getting contacts apply, with breaking in even more accepted on repeaters than HF.

VHF and UHF FM simplex activity is less than it used to be but is more fulfilling than repeaters as it's your station doing all the work. Make particular note of field days, contests and enhanced conditions when activity is likely to be higher. Either call CQ on the published 'calling frequencies' (which are normally quiet enough to continue the contact on them, provided you leave gaps between transmissions) or 'tail-end' stations on other simplex frequencies. The same goes for VHF/UHF SSB except that operators there are more likely to have high-quality equipment, feedlines and antennas and are therefore able to work longer distances.

II CLUBS AND INFORMATION

Joining a radio club is a good way to find out what other amateurs are up to and how you can get the most out of your involvement in amateur radio. Many have licence study courses and run exams if you need to resit your test. Social gatherings, excursions, operating experience and construction projects are other benefits.

Annual club-run hamfests, rallies or flea markets are useful if you need to re-equip your station on a budget, with prices often lower than eBay. If you prefer to ask questions first, there'll be no shortage of advice on equipment to buy or avoid. You may even be able to pick up something suitable from fellow members upgrading their stations.

Small cities typically have one general-interest radio club covering the whole area. Large metropolitan areas often have several, each covering a group of suburbs. They may also be the home of city, state or national special-interest groups promoting facets such as VHF/UHF/microwaves, repeaters, HF contesting or low-power operating.

Club sizes range from large incorporated associations with their own premises to informal social groups that meet at a restaurant, park or beach. The former usually have strong web and social media presence while you may only find out about the latter through word-of-mouth.

Your national amateur radio society's website will have contact details for the larger and more formal clubs. Your area may also have weekly nets and news broadcasts that provide details of meetings, sales and other events. These are typically on VHF/UHF repeaters and possibly also HF frequencies.

National society websites

Amateur Radio Society of India arsi.info
American Radio Relay League arrl.org
Associazione Radioamatori Italiani ari.it
Deutscher Amateur Radio Club darc.de
Experimenterende Danske Radioamatorer edr.dk
Foreningen Sveriges Sandareamatorer ssa.se
Hong Kong Amateur Radio Transmitting Society harts-web.org
Irish Radio Transmitters Society irts.ie
Japan Amateur Radio League jarl.org
Liga de Amadores Brasileiros de Radio Emissao labre.org.br
Malaysian Amateur Radio Transmitters Society marts.org.my
New Zealand Association of Radio Transmitters nzart.org.nz
Organisation Radio Amatir Republik Indonesia orari.or.id
Phillipine Amateur Radio Association para.org.ph
Radio Club Argentino lu4aa.org
Radio Club de Chile ce3aa.cl
Reseau des Emetteurs Francais r-e-f.org
Radio Amateurs Canada wp.rac.ca
Radio Society of Great Britain rsgb.org
Russia Amateur Radio Union srr.ru
Singapore Amateur Radio Transmitting Society sarts.org.sg
Union de Radioaficionados Espanoles ure.es
Union Schweizerischer Kurzwellen Amateure uska.ch
Vereninging voor Experimenteel Radio Onderzoek in Nederland veron.nl
Wireless Institute of Australia wia.org.au

The national societies listed above often also produce a magazine whose columns and articles give a good view of today's amateur activities. As mentioned earlier, they also provide other services and represent amateurs to government on regulatory matters.

Geographically remote or can't get to a club meeting? Consider asking questions on an online forum or group. Those on qrz.com and eham.net are the biggest but there are also country-based and specialist forums. They carry some great answers and informative discussions worth saving or bookmarking. Facebook groups are even more popular and exist for most aspects of amateur radio.

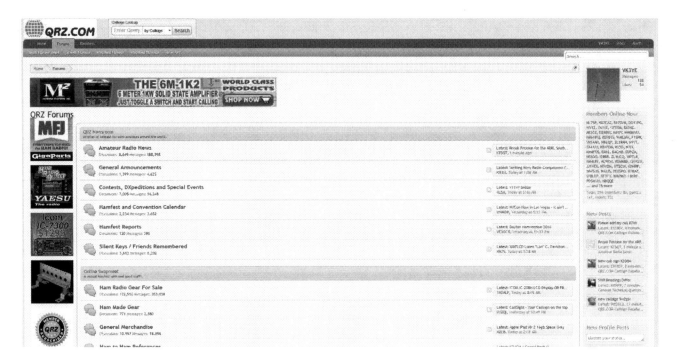

Social media has its dark side, though. Like the village market, participants comprise a cross-section of humanity, including know-it-alls, bigots, inarticulates, the short-fused, the backward and the socially challenged. Post count does not equal technical expertise. And technical expertise does not equal social maturity.

It's amazing how some who behave acceptably on the air or in person become abrasive trolls online. Nasty comments reflect more on the writer than their target. Ignore them and don't let them affect either you personally or your interest in radio.

At the same time, there are things that returnees (or newcomers) with questions can do to make the forum experience more pleasant for everyone, including those trying to help. These include:

- Use the forum's search function to find past discussions on a topic you wish to know more about. Your exact question may have already been answered.
- Search Google for the answer before asking. Again, there is a high chance others have had similar questions answered.
- Mention the prior steps you took to find an answer when you do ask a question. Replies will be better if respondents can see you've made an effort first.
- Specific questions get the best answers. A broad question like 'what is the best HF antenna' requires a book-length answer that no one will write. Whereas stating preferred bands and distances, available space and cost requirements should elicit useful answers.
- Respect readers' and respondents' time. This means writing clearly, spelling well and rereading before posting. Results will be better this way.

Without formal vetting of forum posts, answers received will vary in suitability and accuracy. A lot of nonsense is sprouted on antennas, for instance. Someone may claim something 'works' but their definition of this might be signals substantially weaker than those achieved with a common dipole. Other replies may be from perfectionists with professional or engineering backgrounds. Their responses may be technically correct but could prove discouraging if their recommendations exceed available

GETTING BACK INTO AMATEUR RADIO

space and budget. Consequently forums should supplement your reading rather than be your sole source of information.

QRZ and Eham cover many general amateur radio topics. They also have sub-forums for particular facets. There are also many other active local or special-interest groups online. These typically use a Facebook group or Yahoo Groups email list. Search these out if you want detailed information on amateur activity in a particular area or specialist activity.

As well as replying to forum posts, amateurs are also enthusiastic writers and video producers. The web and YouTube is full of articles and videos on all facets of amateur radio. Mine are vk3ye.com and youtube.com/vk3ye respectively. Also, if you hear or work someone interesting on the air, type in their call sign at qrz.com. Chances are they will have an informative profile describing their station or projects.

93

12 CONCLUSION

The basic ethos of amateur radio is largely similar to what it was years ago. However the way we do it has changed dramatically. Much of this has been due to technological developments that have made established ham activities easier and paved the way for new modes.

As a returning amateur, you should not be daunted by getting up to speed with these changes. Be assured that the satisfaction achieved is well worth trying the new challenges of various facets of amateur radio.

13 AMATEUR RADIO ACRONYMS

AF: audio frequency
AM: amplitude modulation (voice transmitting mode)
APRS: automatic position reporting system
CQ: general call to any station
CW: continuous wave / Morse code (transmitting mode)
DMR: Digital Mobile Radio (a digital voice mode)
DSB: double sideband (voice transmitting mode)
DSTAR: Digital Smart Technologies for Amateur Radio (a digital voice mode)
DX: long distance (also DXer – someone who contacts long distance stations)
EMR: electromagnetic radiation
FM: frequency modulation (transmitting mode)
HF: high frequencies (3 to 30 MHz)
IF: intermediate frequency
IOTA: islands of the air (operating activity)
IRLP: Internet Repeater Linking Project
LF: low frequencies (30 to 300 kHz)
LSB: lower sideband (see single sideband)
MF: medium frequencies (300 kHz to 3MHz)
PSK: phase shift keying (digital transmitting mode)
QRM: man-made interference (Q-code)
QRN: natural interference (Q-code)
QRP: low power transmitting
QRZ: who is calling me? (Q-code)
QSB: signal fading (Q-code)
QSL: confirmation of transmission or contact (Q-code)
QSO: contact (Q-code)
RF: radio frequency
RIT: receiver incremental tuning (i.e. fine tuning)
RST: readability/strength/tone (signal report method)
RTTY: radio teletype
SDR: software defined radio
SFI: solar flux index (propagation)
SOTA: summits of the air (operating activity)
SSB: single sideband (voice transmitting mode)
SSTV: slow-scan television (transmitting mode)
SWR: standing wave ratio. Same as VSWR (voltage standing wave ratio)
UHF: ultra-high frequencies (300 to 3000 MHz)
USB: upper sideband (see single sideband)
VHF: very high frequencies (30 to 300 MHz)
WSJT: weak signal digital transmitting mode
WSPR: weak signal propagation reporter (slow speed transmitting mode)
73: best wishes

14 ABOUT THE AUTHOR

Peter (mis?)spent his youth at rubbish tips, taking apart given radios and TVs and building electronic projects that mostly did not work. He avoided soldering until figuring out that new solder on a shiny tip works better than reusing solder gathered from the chassis of vacuum tube radios.

Milestones included the construction of a crystal set, discovering shortwave broadcasting on a tube receiver and making a simple 'electronic organ' from a Dick Smith Fun Way book. Hours were spent putting wires into springs on a Tandy 150-in-1 electronics set. Amazingly some wires could be pulled out and the project would still sort of work with only half the parts in circuit.

Two back-to-back AM/shortwave radios led to the discovery of amateur SSB activity and a novice licence. The following year was spent building transmitters no one heard. A one-tube crystal-controlled CW transmitter from the 1973 ARRL Handbook provided the first contacts – mostly CW/SSB cross-mode on the 3.579 MHz TV colour burst crystal frequency. The value of frequency agility was an early lesson and various VFOs were built, most of them drifty.

Further construction enabled more bands, more modes and smaller gear. Projects included a 7 MHz VXO CW direct conversion transceiver, a 2 metre FM portable transceiver, and a 14 MHz CW transmitter for Cycle 22, then near its peak. Later favourites included HF DSB and SSB transceivers (often using ceramic resonators, ladder crystal filters, NE602s and BD139 transistors) and phasing SSB equipment.

Limited space led to experiments with magnetic loops and HF pedestrian mobile. The joys of the latter (along with the perils of a trailing counterpoise) were first discovered with a converted Johnson Viking CB on 28 MHz. This was mounted in a carpeted chipboard box with battery and 1.5 metre whip. A move to a beachside suburb brought further HF portable and pedestrian mobile activity which remains an interest to this day.

Peter is a prolific writer and video producer with items on the web and YouTube.

.

I5 THANKS

Thank you for reading.

I invite you to share your comments and thoughts on one or more of the following:

Facebook (search for 'VK3YE Radio Books')

Goodreads

Twitter

Constructive feedback would also be appreciated.

16 OTHER BOOKS BY VK3YE

Minimum QRP: Doing more with under five watt amateur radio contains tested strategies for low-power success on the HF bands. Equipment, antennas and operating are all covered in detail. Its crafty tips for working the most with the least should become more valuable as solar activity declines in the next few years.

Minimum QRP is for a broad worldwide audience. Newcomers, the more experienced and those returning to amateur radio are already benefiting from its contents with brisk sales since its release.

Minimum QRP is exclusively available as a Kindle e-book. You can read it on a portable e-reader, your home PC or other device. Packed with more than 200 pages of information, it's yours for under $US5 or equivalent.

Further details, including a table of contents, list of reviews and ordering information can be found at vk3ye.com or by searching the title on amazon.com

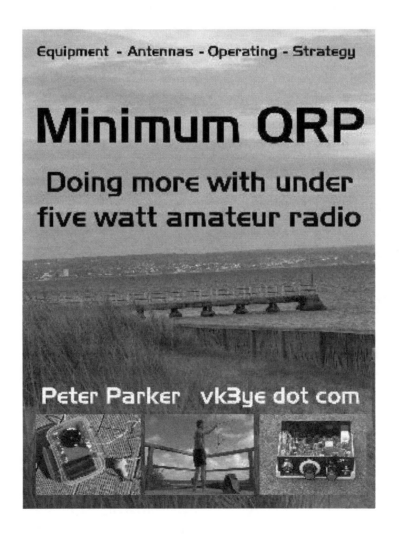

Hand-carried QRP antennas is the book that takes the mystery out of portable antennas. After inviting you to assess your needs, it discusses the pros and cons of popular types. Its style is straightforward and practical with almost no maths.

Many ideas for cheap but good materials suitable for portable antennas are given. Beginners and those returning to radio after a break should especially find this advice handy.

Finally there are construction details on a variety of simple but practical antennas and accessories suitable for portable operating. All have been built and tested by the author over almost 30 years of successful QRP activity.

Hand-carried QRP antennas is an e-book readable on most devices (free software available if you don't have a Kindle). It is Peter's second book, following on from the popular *Minimum QRP*, released in 2015.

Further details, including a table of contents, list of reviews and ordering information can be found at vk3ye.com or by searching the title on amazon.com

For news on these and future books, please subscribe to VK3YE Radio Books on Facebook or VK3YE's channel on YouTube.

.

Notes

Made in the USA
San Bernardino, CA
10 March 2019